The ABC
of Soccer Sense

Strategy & Tactics today

The ABC of Soccer Sense

Strategy & Tactics today

Tommy Docherty

Arco Publishing Company, Inc New York

Published by Arco Publishing Company, Inc.
219 Park Avenue South, New York, N.Y. 10003

Printed in Great Britain

Library of Congress Cataloging in Publication Data

Docherty, Thomas Henderson.
  ABC of soccer sense.

  1. Soccer coaching.   I. Title.
GV943.8.D62   796.33'42   78-2844
ISBN 0-668-04627-9

Contents

Introduction   6

1   Ideal Players   7

2   Fitness and Training   23

3   Strategy   54

4   Tactics   74

5   Captains and Substitutes
    Home and Away Tactics   95

6   Outstanding Club Sides   104

7   Outstanding International Sides   122

8   World Cup '78   138

Index   142

Introduction

Football, planned and played properly, is a simple game. Only people too deeply cemented in theory and not enough in practice complicate it.

There has been a lot of damaging mumbo jumbo talked about the game by alleged experts who seem to think that football is best played with a piece of chalk on a blackboard.

The game has been my life for more than thirty years and I have learnt in that time that football is as easy as ABC . . .

A for APPLICATION. You will get the best results, whether it is as a player or as a coach, by applying yourself to the sometimes tedious but very necessary job of learning the basic techniques of every aspect of the game.

B for BELIEF. You must have total belief in your ability to master the arts of soccer. This will come automatically if you *apply* yourself properly.

C for CHARACTER. I have seen many players with wonderful God-given footballing talent wreck their careers simply because they have not had the character to survive the pressures that the game can heap on you. The greatest players – the likes of Pele, Beckenbauer, Bobby Charlton, di Stefano – have one thing in common: unshakeable self discipline that has always helped them conquer the crises that can confront you in the highly-competitive world of football.

In this book my aim is to take the student of soccer on an uncomplicated path through what can be a maze of football theory. I shall give a total breakdown of every aspect of the game so that the strategy and tactics of modern soccer can be easily understood and put into practice.

There have been many coaching manuals published in the past, some of them so complex that the authors have trapped their readers in a web of confusion.

I have endeavoured to be as clear and concise as possible about every point in the game and hope that whether you are new to soccer or an old friend that you will find this book as easy to follow and understand as ABC.

I wish you many happy hours of involvement with the greatest game on earth.

Tommy Docherty

1
Ideal Players

In my role as a Football League manager, I have spent more than £3-million in a constant search for the *ideal* players. But even with unlimited resources in the transfer market, the right man is not always available.

The 'right' player for a specific role in a team does not necessarily have to cost a fortune. Team building is all about getting the composition of a side right, fitting the pieces together like a jigsaw until eleven individuals lock together in a single unit. In this opening chapter I want to deal with what makes the ideal player and to look at the demands and responsibilities of each position on the pitch.

Footballers come in all shapes and sizes. England once had an international goalkeeper called Billy Foulke who stood 6 ft 3 in and weighed 21 stones (294 pounds). Billy Bremner, who captained Scotland when I was in charge of the Scottish International Team, was just over 5 ft 4 in tall and barely topped 10 stones (140 pounds), yet was as determined and dynamic a player as I have ever seen.

It's not the size of the player that counts as much as his ability and application. Billy Wright was once told he was too small for football, but he was big enough to play 105 times for England and captained them in 90 matches. Celtic sold me to Preston back in 1949 because they thought that at 5 ft 7 in I was too small to develop into a dominating player. I later won 25 international caps and skippered Scotland and Arsenal.

Pele, the king of football, stands only 5 ft 10 in but became a giant of the game because of his phenomenal skill that made defenders look dwarfs alongside him when he was in full flow.

If you are in the process of team building, you should be searching for a blend of strength and skill and a mixture of youth and experience. The most difficult job of all for a manager or a coach is to obtain the correct balance. I have managed sides that have been brimming with talented individual players but they have failed to mould together as a team. Yet there have been many instances of ordinary players fitting together to make great teams that had the balance just right.

By no stretch of the imagination could the Southampton team that beat Manchester United in the 1976 FA Cup Final be described as having been over-endowed with outstanding players. But they got it altogether as a team, all of them working with maximum effort and industry to cancel out the extra skill

Pele…a giant of the game who had phenomenal skill and perfect poise and balance even when at full pace.

factor that was a feature of my Manchester United side.

When I moved from Manchester United to Derby, Brian Clough had just steered Nottingham Forest back to the First Division. They were the early-season pacemakers and many people in the game sneered that they were 'five-minute wonders'. It was not until they had stretched their lead at the top of the table to six points early in 1978 that people at last began to concede that they were championship class.

The secret of that Forest side was their *togetherness*. They concentrated on doing the simple things well and had the necessary foundation of a sound and solid defence. Forest were a great advertisement for the point that I shall keep emphasizing in this book: *football is as simple as ABC*.

The England team of the mid-1960s had only three world-class players in Gordon Banks, Bobby Moore and Bobby Charlton. But because everybody played for each other and put selfish motives second to the needs of the team they became world champions, despite the fact that sides in the 1966 tournament such as Hungary, Portugal and the Argentine had classier individual players.

A point I want to make very forcibly is that team organization is vital if you intend to be consistent over a season, *but don't over-organize to the point where you might be stifling the creative artistry of a player with outstanding ability.* You must leave room for freedom of expression inside the framework of an organized team effort. Let us take each position in turn and analyse just what goes into making the ideal player.

8

Goalkeepers

Ideally you want your goalkeeper to be somewhere about six feet tall. There have been several notable exceptions but generally the greatest goalkeepers are big men. Players whose names roll off the tongue like old friends – Lev Yashin, Frank Swift, Bert Trautmann, Gordon Banks – have all been goalkeeping goliaths.

Alan Hodgkinson and Eddie Hopkinson, former England international goalkeepers, were both 5 ft 9 in tall but made up for their short stature by having tremendous spring and agility.

The goalkeeper is a key man in any team. He knows he can undo the work of ten men with just one moment's lapse of concentration or just the slightest error. A single mistake can be cruelly punished. Your goalkeeper therefore needs a strong temperament so that he can quickly compose himself should anything go wrong. I have seen good teams fall apart because their goalkeeper's nerves have been wrecked by a simple handling error.

A goalkeeper must have the right mental approach. He needs courage, quick reflexes, the confidence and authority to command his goal area and total concentration

I shall go into detail in a later chapter on how coaching can help develop a goalkeeper's technique to handle shots and crosses with confidence.

If I could put a perfect goalkeeper together from all the finest players of the modern game, I think I would go for the catching ability of Peter Bonetti, the reflexes of Alex Stepney, the composure of Sepp Maier, the agility of Ray Clemence, the courage of Bob Wilson, the professionalism of Dino Zoff, the application of Peter Shilton and the positioning judgment of Gordon Banks. Pat Jennings has all these qualities and is as near perfect as you can get. Sometimes a player is born to be a great goalkeeper, but more often he is manufactured. By the correct training methods, a fair goalkeeper can become a safe and reliable last line of defence. The hardest thing to teach him is the knowledge and judgment of when to leave the goal-line. At even the highest level of international football you see goals given away by a goalkeeper's reluctance to leave his line to cut an angle or collect a high ball.

Even the greatest goalkeepers can get their angles wrong. Ray Clemence, for whom I have a very high regard, made a marginal error that cost Liverpool the FA Cup in the memorable 1977 Final against my Manchester United team at Wembley.

Clemence advanced from his line to cut down the target at which Stuart Pearson was aiming but he made the mistake of leaving his near post unguarded and Pearson beat him with a low killer shot that just squeezed into the net. The Liverpool and England goalkeeper had been brutally punished for being no more than a foot the wrong way on his positioning.

There are some over-rated goalkeepers that I would not trust with my best china, but one who never lets his side down is Pat Jennings, now with Arsenal after giving marvellous service to Tottenham. But for Jennings, I feel Manchester City would have been last season's League Cup winners. His performance in the sixth round tie at Maine Road was out of this world, and proved that a goalkeeper has the power to change the entire course and pattern of a game. On a count of chances created, Manchester City were at least three goals superior to Arsenal. Jennings pulled off five superb saves, three of them in the 'impossible' category. His performance inspired the whole Arsenal team and they produced extra effort to hold out for a draw and a replay at Highbury which they eventually won. Jennings has got goal-keeping down to a fine art. He does it with a minimum of fuss and always puts safety first. One of the 'hidden' strengths of his game is his concentration.

A goalkeeper must 'live' every kick in a match so that he is totally alert and tuned-in when the action switches to his goal area. It is a cardinal sin for a goalkeeper to lose his concentration. Even in his idle moments he must take an interest in what is happening on the pitch, even if the ball is 100 yards away in the opposition penalty area. I have seen goalkeepers with great physical powers fail to make the grade in professional football simply because they lack the mental alertness that is vital for all of the 90 minutes of a match.

Another important aspect of goalkeeping that I shall go into in greater depth later in the book is distribution. The alert goalkeeper can launch a successful counter attack by quickly getting the ball to an unmarked colleague. Equally, the goalkeeper who doesn't think and act quickly can often put his defence under pressure by a poorly placed ball. *It is imperative that a goalkeeper should work at becoming as accurate and imaginative with his distribution as any outfield player.*

Goalkeepers need specialized training, particularly in the company of the back-four defenders who will play in front of him. They must accept him as the master or the boss of the goal area, following his calls and instructions until a deep understanding and confidence has been cemented. Above all a goal-keeper must have concentration and confidence. The old proverb 'He who hesitates is lost' could have been written with goalkeepers in mind. A hesitant goalkeeper can undermine an entire team.

The goalkeeping points on which I shall concentrate in the chapter on training methods are: (1) Handling; (2) Positioning; (3) Distribution; (4) Command; (5) Penalties.

Full-backs

The full-back's role has changed dramatically over the last 20 years. He used to be essentially a defender with the sole job of guarding his goal against attacks from the wing. Now he is much more of an all-rounder whose chief responsibility is still to defend his own goal but with the added demands of becoming an auxiliary attacker when his team is applying the pressure. Over-lapping runs made by a full-back at the right time can be a destructive weapon for a team. But they can be suicidal if unleashed without discretion or concentration.

The great modern full-backs such as Berti Vogts, Paul Breitner, Ze Maria of Brazil, Wim Suurbier, Rudi Krol, Francisco Marinho and Giacinto Facchetti are all masters of attacking play but never go forward at the expense of their defence. I rated converted winger Terry Cooper one of the most creative attacking full-backs I have ever seen but his defensive strategy was often exposed because he was so intent on going forward that he left acres of space for his opponents to exploit. I particularly remember the way his defensive deficiencies were exposed by Celtic's Jimmy Johnstone when Leeds played the Scottish champions in the 1970 European Cup semi-final. Johnstone continually left the Leeds defence in ruins with twisting, tormenting runs that gave Cooper nightmares. In fairness to Cooper, Johnstone on his form of that two-leg match would have turned any full-back inside out and it was thanks mainly to his skill that Celtic went through to the European Cup Final at the expense of Leeds.

A full-back is fundamentally a marker, a player whose job it is to win the ball and then use it to trigger a counter attack. *He must be a master of tackling technique, ball control and, above all, positional play.* The role he plays in a game is often dictated by the opposition. If the opposing team is playing without wingers, he should be alert to overlapping runs from his rival full-back and also to making a positive contribution to his own team's attacking moves.

I like to think that, while manager of Manchester United, I played some part in bringing wingers back into British football. I am a great believer in mounting attacks down the flanks; the full-backs who faced United, playing the way I used to order them to play, always knew they were going to have their hands full with the flying wing wizardry of Steve Coppell and Gordon Hill.

To counter the menace of a flying winger, a full-back must be quick on the turn, able to jockey and mark tightly without commiting himself to a tackle, and fast to recover if he has been caught napping. It was these qualities in young Steve Buckley that prompted me to bring him to Derby from Luton Town for £160,000. David Nish, a highly competent and capable full-back, was plagued by a knee injury and I saw in Steve all the right ingredients for the *ideal* full-back. So I fitted him into my Derby jigsaw as a replacement piece while David Nish concentrated on trying to regain full fitness.

When selecting full-backs, you must look for ideal partners. George Cohen and Ray Wilson went together like bacon and eggs for England. Each was always aware of his partner's position and they had a telepathic understanding of when the time was right to strike forward, knowing that the other one would take the responsibility to cover in emergency. Danny McGrain, one of the greatest of all modern full-backs, had rewarding partnerships for Scotland with Sandy Jardine and Willie Donachie. McGrain has not only the intelligence and the skill to do his own job with great expertise, but also the assurance and team-awareness to help bring out the best in his partner, giving encouragement and advice in the heat of battle. McGrain is a model full-back who is always positive when going forward and resilient when under pressure. His tackling is timed to perfection.

Tackling is an art all of its own. A full-back — any defender for that matter — must learn when and where to commit himself to the tackle. Only fools rush in before they have properly positioned themselves. A mistimed tackle can cost a goal. Better to stand off and restrict the movement of the player in possession than gamble with a tackle that could miss. *The best full-backs know when and, even more important, when not to tackle.*

There was a time when the popular image of a full-back was that he should be a hefty, immobile man who tackled like a tank, be more interested in distance than direction when hoofing the ball away, and should consider the opposition half of the pitch forbidden territory. The modern full-back aims to be as fast as any forward, meticulous with his passing and to have the stamina to make as many runs as necessary deep into the opponents' half of the field.

The really progressive full-back will play a thinking man's game. He will weigh up the strengths and weaknesses of the opponent he is delegated to mark and adjust his tactics accordingly. Before a ball is kicked he will have learned as much as possible about such points as whether his opponent is strongest on his right or left foot, whether he prefers hugging the touchline or moving inside to make his run and whether the main weapon in his armoury is speed or ball skill.

He must be disciplined into putting the requirements of the team effort first. His positioning will be influenced to a great extent by the problems and per-formances of his team-mates. When up against a team playing without wingers, for instance, his main work could be as a support player to the central defenders should they be under intense pressure. He must always be aware of what his full-back partner is doing and ensure that never in a game are they both caught stranded upfield on attacking runs.

The full-back's role in modern football is much more varied and exacting than it used to be and the responsibilities and demands are greater. It means there is more scope for a player with imagination and vision but he must never forget that his prime purpose is to defend the goal. I shall take a much wider look at the functions of a full-back within the framework of organized team formations in the chapter on strategy.

Central Defenders

The two players who stand in the middle of the back line of the defence are the kings of the castle. When they are toppled, your team is in trouble.

Ideally both players should be tall so that they can be commanding in the air. If they are below six feet, they need excellent positional sense and a goal-keeper behind them who can carry the responsibility for gathering the high balls.

Many great defences have been built around giant, dominating centre-halves. England's 1966 World Cup winners had big Jackie Charlton, with Bobby Moore supreme in a supporting role alongside him. Barry Hulshoff was a strongly-built, decisive centre-half who played a prominent part in the 1970s successes of Ajax and Holland, and Derby emerged as a power in the English First Division thanks largely to the authority in the air of Roy McFarland who was effectively in harness with the small but shrewd Colin Todd.

In the absence of a giant to dominate the middle of the defence, you can get players to work to an adaption of the traditional centre-half role. The 1977 FA Cup Final gave a prime example of this when neither Manchester United nor Liverpool played with a recognized centre-half.

United had Brian Greenhoff and Martin Buchan, both under six feet tall, operating together in the middle of the back line. Both are useful but not devastating in the air. They worked superbly well with Alex Stepney, leaving him to cope with the high crosses while they concentrated on tight-marking the nearest Liverpool opponent. Greenhoff is an intelligent positional player

Point of Law…not all attempts to win the ball turn out to be legal. Ray Macfarland in action against Chelsea.

Missed it…Colin Todd's attempt to win this ball was, unusually for Todd, unsuccessful.

and fiercely competitive. He can shape the pattern of play from the back with imaginative distribution. Buchan's strength is in his quick reading of situations that enables him to be a thought and a move ahead of rival forwards.

Liverpool had Tommy Smith and Emlyn Hughes as their central defenders, both of whom knew they could rely on Ray Clemence to cover for them in the air. Both were suspect if you could attack them down their left side, but had such good positional sense and recovery powers that they were able to knit together tightly under the severest pressure.

The sole objective of your two centre-backs is to defend and protect your goal. *It is a bonus if they are able to invade the opposition penalty area and use their height to force goals from set situations, but they must never lose sight of their chief responsibility which is to bring strength and stability to the defence.* The centre-back who rushes blindly forward and becomes stranded during a counter attack by the opposition is letting his team down in a novice-like way.

Watch the best centre-backs in action and you will see they work together like a tandem team. One will take responsibility for the right-hand side of the pitch and the other will patrol the left. They will always cover for each other in emergency and work in close liaison with the goalkeeper whose calling from the back will decide who is to take the high ball.

Their method of play — the timing of tackles and their contribution to attacking movements — is obviously influenced by the team tactics. I shall go into the sweeper system in the strategy chapter but if there is nobody sweeping up at the back then clearly the two central defenders must play a strictly disciplined game and take few risks. I shall also take a close look at the zonal and man-to-man marking systems both of which make different demands on the central defenders.

Centre-backs have to be quick thinkers, have the vision to know what is happening around them and the judgment to know when they are best occupied away from the all-important central base. They must be alert to strikers making decoy runs aimed at luring them from the middle of the defence to make space for a team-mate.

Intelligent distribution by your central defenders can be a match-winning factor. They get a lot of possession simply because they are at the heart of the action. Properly placed passes to colleagues in space can spark goal-making movements that catch the opposition with their defences down. The two masters of this counter-puncing ploy in recent years have been Franz Beckenbauer and Bobby Moore.

Beckenbauer continually set up a conveyor belt of passes from his sweeper base behind the German back line, often coming through himself to exchange one-twos with attacking team-mates. Moore's favourite attacking weapon was a long right-footed pass upfield to a team-mate running into space, a tactic he got down to a fine art when Geoff Hurst was his running mate.

The centre-back must be prepared to accept responsibility because he must act on snap decisions that can be severely punished if wrong. He should have a total knowledge of the principles of defensive play, particularly those of tackling and marking.

Midfield

Now we come to the 'engine-room' of any team, the midfield, where matches are won and lost according to the contribution of three or sometimes four players.

The modern midfield man comes in three different packages. There is the stunningly skilful and creative type who can destroy a defence with one paralysing pass. These are in the mould of artists like Gunther Netzer, Jovan Acimovic of Yugoslavia, Carlos Babington of Argentina, Machado Octavio of Portugal, Wolfgang Overath, Wim Van Henegem, Gianni Rivera and Gerson, the architect of Brazil's 1970 World Cup victory. The greatest exponents of this type of highly-skilled midfield play in English League football in recent years have been Bobby Charlton, Johnny Giles and Ian Callaghan, all of them past masters who served their early apprenticeships as wingers.

Then there is the energetic all-purpose player who causes problems to the opposition with a mixture of invention and industry. Lou Macari is as good an example of this type of grafter as I can think of. He is competitive, passes with accuracy and imagination, is a sharp finisher in the box and willingly runs back deep into his own half to win the ball and help the defence when they are under pressure. Macari and Sammy McIlroy were the twin engines that helped drive Manchester United to the 1977 FA Cup Final at Wembley.

The third type of modern midfield man is inclined to be more combative. He is a challenger and a hustler, winning the ball for his team and then releasing it to players better equipped for creative work. Billy Bremner typified this kind

The competitors...it is crucial that midfield players should be competitive if they are to gain control of their territory. Gerry Daly (left) and Lou Macari are two midfield terriers who will never concede an inch.

of player in the early 1960s, but had the skill to add a new dimension to his game later in his career. West Ham would never have won the FA Cup in 1975 without the power-propelling in midfield of Billy Bonds, and Peter Storey certainly made his mark with the Arsenal double-winning team of 1970–71. Storey performed his task so well that Alf Ramsey gave him the job that Nobby Stiles had carried out with such driving force in the 1966 World Cup tournament.

Your midfield line-up naturally depends on which formation you are playing. This must be decided by your playing strength and also by the strengths and weaknesses of the opposition. I personally don't like the 4-4-2 set-up because it is too defensively based, but there are times when your tactics and player availability demand such an approach. My preference is for a freer, more fluent 4-3-3 or 4-2-4 formation, and it is inside these frameworks that you rely heavily on the skill and industry of the midfield players.

The best midfield players work together as a team within a team. They are always on the look out to make supporting runs for each other and accept that their main function is to feed the strikers with correctly-weighted passes that are penetrative without being predictable. *Good ball control and an ability to pass the ball accurately for distances up to 40 yards are imperative for the midfield player who wants to stamp his authority on a game.* He should also work at perfecting his shooting so that he is able to snap up the chances that often come his way on the edge of the penalty area.

Ideally, you want a strong right-footed player to patrol the right side of the midfield and a left-footed player to operate on the left. Liverpool came up with a well-balanced pairing with the emergence of Jimmy Case and Ray Kennedy. Case advanced from the right, eager to pounce on any loose ball with a thundering shot and Kennedy's skilled left-foot work provided Liverpool with width as well as striking power.

A midfield anchorman must perfect the art of tackling because his main role is to break down opposition attacks and then make quick and intelligent use of the ball. Super fitness is crucial for all midfield players as they have to cover acres of ground, acting as the link between defence and attack and as defenders or attackers as the play dictates.

One of the most productive midfield trios of modern times was the combination of Howard Kendall, Alan Ball and Colin Harvey that steered Everton to the League Championship in 1969–70, winning by a staggering margin of nine points from runners-up Leeds. Kendall, Ball and Harvey gave a perfect demonstration of how the midfield men should work together. All were skilful and industrious and always willing to put the needs of the team first. They attacked with zest, covered for each other in moments of crisis and scooted back to base the second their attacking work had been completed. They were the great dictators of Goodison and proved that a League title could be won from midfield.

Soon after my arrival at Derby County I brought together a midfield trio in the Ball-Kendall-Harvey class. Gerry Daly was already there, having transferred to Derby from Manchester United while I was manager at Old Trafford. I had always been an admirer of Daly's intelligent and imaginative play and it was never my wish that he should leave United, so I was delighted to catch up

Gerry Daly... surrounded by Everton players but showing the determination that has made him such a key man in midfield for Derby.

with him again at Derby. I then transplanted the heart of the Scottish World Cup team into the Derby midfield by buying Don Masson from Queen's Park Rangers and Bruce Rioch from Everton.

They were like 'The Three Scrooges' in midfield, giving nothing away to the opposition. Their high work rate, pin-pointed passing and sheer skill and enthusiasm raised the standards and performances of all their team-mates and confirmed my opinion that a good midfield trio can 'make' a team.

A few miles down the road, Nottingham Forest were also buzzing in midfield thanks largely to the efforts of two ex-Derby stalwarts, John McGovern and Archie Gemmill. They combined with Martin O'Neill to give Forest midfield drive and direction, a dual role they had once successfully performed for Derby when County won the championship during the eventful Brian Clough era at the Baseball Ground. It had been my strictly personal view that Gemmill had fallen into the habit of carrying the ball for too long a time and distance at critical moments in a match, but he started to release the ball at the right time with Forest, and once again stood out as an *ideal* midfield player.

Strikers

Successful strikers get the goals and the glory. But if they are not putting the ball into the net they get the axe. No team can afford the luxury of a non-scoring striker.

Scoring goals is at the same time the most difficult yet most stimulating and rewarding job in football. There is so much that goes into the breeding of a top

17

striker: skill, shooting power and accuracy, courage, quickness of thought and action, opportunism, speed and manoeuvrability in restricted space and the vision to see openings a split second before anybody else. Only the greatest players are gifted with all these attributes. Pele, Cruyff and di Stefano, the most talented all-round footballers there have ever been, had them. So too did the likes of Jimmy Greaves, Denis Law and George Best.

So much planning now goes into the stopping of goals that the scoring of them has become harder than ever before. *You need a balance of strength and skill in your striking force, players who know the best positions to take up the moment your team makes a forward advance and who can control the ball under severe challenges from rival defenders.*

The striker who wants to make a success of his job must be prepared to work overtime on his close ball control, acceleration from a standing start, shooting accuracy with either foot, passing under pressure and improving his positional awareness. A lot of attention must also be given to head work, concentrating on getting plenty of lift for the power header and direction for the glancing header.

Great strikers often come in pairs. Greaves used to feed eagerly off the battering-ram tactics of Bobby Smith, a centre-forward of the old school who put power before finesse. Their styles were as alike as grass and granite yet they fitted perfectly together.

Geoff Hurst and Roger Hunt were always happy in harness together, making intelligent runs off the ball as they unselfishly worked at creating space for each other. *The ability to unhinge a defence by working off the ball is*

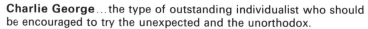

Charlie George...the type of outstanding individualist who should be encouraged to try the unexpected and the unorthodox.

another crucial area in which the top strikers must excel. It is often thankless work that goes unnoticed by the spectators but is vital to the team effort.

Hurst, a model striker, had another fine understanding with Johnny 'Budgie' Byrne for West Ham in the early 1960s. Byrne was the elegant 'touch' player while Hurst supplied the power and the punch.

Manchester United's success in 1977 was due to a large extent to the quick understanding struck up between Stuart Pearson and Jimmy Greenhoff following Jimmy's arrival from Stoke City. They complemented each other with their quickness and sharpness of mind and their radar-like instinct for knowing the positions each should find to make the most of a situation.

These prolific partnerships do not just happen. The players spend hours working in training at getting everything right. Kevin Keegan and John Toshack went together like whisky and soda for Liverpool. The positions they took up that were so disturbing to defences were well rehearsed movements that had been perfected only after hours of hard graft in training sessions. There is a four-letter word that every successful striker knows well. To get to the top and stay there they have to *work*.

I had always been led to understand that the word 'work' was missing from the vocabulary of Charlie George, but I had no complaints about his team and training efforts when I took over as his manager at Derby. There have been few more gifted forwards in post-war British football than this cocky but likeable Cockney. He is equally efficient and menacing as an out-and-out striker or when lying back just behind the front line. One of his greatest assets is the ability to shoot a ball at great pace and power almost without any backlift. I gave Charlie a free rein at Derby because he is the type of outstanding individualist who can win a match with one explosive moment of magic.

He is the kind of creative artist that we have been stifling in British football by *over*-organizing teams and not allowing players of talent the freedom to express themselves. This type of player must be made to recognize that he has a duty to give a 100 per cent contribution to the team effort but should not have too many restrictions placed on his positioning.

If you are seeking to play positive football, you should encourage players of outstanding ability to try the unexpected and the unorthodox. This way your play will not become stereotyped, and there is every chance that you will be able to confuse even a well-organized defensive side.

Wingers

Anybody who followed my career at Manchester United will know that I have what amounts almost to an obsession about wingers. I am convinced they have a part to play in the modern game even though it is an adjusted and more demanding role than in the pre-1960s. Perhaps my love for wingers stems from the days when I played for Preston behind the man who to this day I consider the greatest British player of all time: Tom Finney.

Gentleman Tom was so versatile that he could play in any forward position and destroy defences with his ball control, speed and body swerve. But it was as a winger that he was at his most effective and created scores of goals with precise centres after turning his full-back inside out with dribbling runs at

Stanley Matthews...the wizard of dribble whose deceptive changes of pace and direction made him one of the greatest wingers of all time.

Tom Finney...one of the all-time greats.

Steve Coppell & Gordon Hill, two of the very best wingers in the modern game.

sprint speed. The only player I have seen to get near his all-round skill is George Best but tragically he did not have Finney's character or commitment.

Those days when wingers would patrol the touchline for 90 minutes are of course over. *But their main function continues to be to bring width to the attack by taking on the full-back and then getting the ball into the middle where the central strikers will have been seeking space for a shot or a header.*

I still maintain that direct wing play is the best way to get round the back of defences. There are of course other ploys, but a fast and clever winger can do the job quickest and most effectively of all.

Wingers must now play a more withdrawn game, accepting their burden of the work in midfield and tracking back to their own penalty area with an overlapping full-back. They must go in search of the ball, not wait for it to be served to them on a plate as used to happen with traditional wingers. They must also share the goal-scoring responsibilities and so therefore in training should give a lot of time to shooting practice.

Today's winger has to be an all-rounder who should be well versed in defensive duties, but his chief chore will be to create goals. Steve Coppell and Gordon Hill were perfect examples of the *ideal* type of modern wingers during my days at Manchester United. Both are able to dribble at full speed with the inside or outside of the foot and even under a strong challenge can send a measured pass to the near post or the far post, which ever is the most appropriate in any given situation. This takes hours of practice. Coppell and Hill sweat buckets in training even though they are established stars. They are always working at perfecting their centres, particularly when in full stride and under pressure from a defender. I had no hesitation in taking Gordon Hill from Manchester United to Derby when he became available because I knew he could give us width and goal thrust.

Novice wingers commit the cardinal sin of running blindly down the touchline with their eyes riveted to the ball and without any idea of what is happening around them. They must keep their heads up and be aware of exactly what their team-mates are doing so that they can make the best possible use of the ball at the time of release.

Sir Alf Ramsey introduced his 'wingless wonders' that won the 1966 World Cup only because he was playing to the strength of the players available to him at the time. He had no intention of wiping wingers off the face of football. With the emergence of outstanding players like Steve Coppell and Peter Barnes, I am hopeful that we can breed a new generation of Tom Finneys and Stanley Matthewses. It will mean better entertainment for the spectators and more variety and spice for the players.

2
Fitness and Training

The preparation for football is as important as the actual playing of the game. Successful teams are rewarded on the pitch for the work they put in off it and in modern soccer correct and concentrated training means the difference between long-term triumph and failure.

Liverpool have been the most successful British club of recent years and they are the perfect example of how specialized training and carefully planned team organization can help put you top of the tree. They became champions of Europe not necessarily because they had the best players but thanks chiefly to them being the best prepared team.

They had the correct balance of what is most appropriately labelled the 'Four-S' success factor:

Strength **S**tamina **S**peed **S**kill

For the best results on the pitch, these must all be practised and perfected in training.

Stamina training

No matter how gifted a player may be, he is committing soccer suicide if he gives less than 100 per cent effort to this vital aspect of fitness preparation.

He will be letting himself and his team down if in the vital late stages of a match he does not have the strength and endurance to continue to give of his best. There is only one way to build stamina and that is through sheer hard work in training.

I recall once reading a quote from Rocky Marciano, the only world heavyweight boxing champion to retire undefeated. He was a fitness fanatic and commented after one of his successful title defences: 'a fighter is only as strong as his legs . . .'.

This quote could be equally attributable to the great footballers. *They must have strength in their legs and stamina in their lungs to keep producing peak effort when match pressures are at their greatest.*

I am not saying that you should build a team of workhorses but it is vital to the overall team performance that all the players are capable of running marathon distances should the necessity arise. The foundation for this strength and stamina must be built during the pre-season training sessions.

At Derby County, this stamina-building work is a gradual process. We start at a fairly gentle pace when the players first report back after the summer break, concentrating on bursts of short-distance running mixed with relaxing long walks, jogging and fundamental body exercises.

Then we get down to the real stamina work with the emphasis on long, daily runs of three to five miles in which the entire squad takes part. It is vital to keep the training programme as varied as possible to avoid any danger of boredom. You can introduce a competitive element, breaking your squad up into small teams and awarding them points for individual placings in races over distances from 50 yards to five miles.

You can also give marks for the circuit training programme when the players will work on a series of set exercises such as press-ups, sit-ups, squat thrusts, standing jumps and running on the spot.

The players will need to push themselves to the edge of exhaustion during these pre-season sessions and you must help them by giving them added interest and incentives. Keep a clock check on their times on runs over set distances and also keep a count of the number of exercises they perform so that they have standards to beat the next day.

Be careful not to push the players past the exhaustion barrier. Too much training can be just as damaging as too little. Remember, it is a *gradual* build-up to peak fitness. Properly organized, each training session should last no longer than two-and-a-half hours at the most. If you let the sessions drag on players can become uninterested and stale.

When picking your pool of players for each training group, try to get a correct balance. Psychology plays a part. Some players might not function properly if placed in a group of, for example, faster runners, or those whose stamina or strength is greater. Age should also be taken into consideration. An 18-year-old youngster will have a different preparation for the season to a 35-year-old veteran. And at Derby County, of course, we have to bear in mind the pressure that may have been placed on players during international tours.

After you have coaxed and encouraged your players through the gruelling but very necessary distance work, gradually switch to quicker interval work. Your players can begin by running 2000 metres in the first session. This is broken down into ten 200-metre stints of fast running with a three-minute rest between each. Increase the distance and cut down on the rest period each day until your players are covering up to 5000 metres in 400-metre bursts with a two-minute rest between each run. Don't let them idle during the rest period. Have plenty of balls on hand so that they can practise their ball skills while waiting for the signal to set off on the next run.

Next on the running schedule after the general stamina build-up work has been completed are the dreaded 'doggies'. We introduced this training method back in my days as manager at Chelsea when Dave Sexton was my coach. Some coaches refer to this type of training stint as 'shuttle running'. The players have nicknamed the runs 'doggies' because they have to race like greyhounds. The shuttle runs really condition a footballer for the sort of sprints he has to make in a match.

From a starting line, five cone markers are placed on the ground a distance of five metres apart and running in a straight line for 25 metres. The players

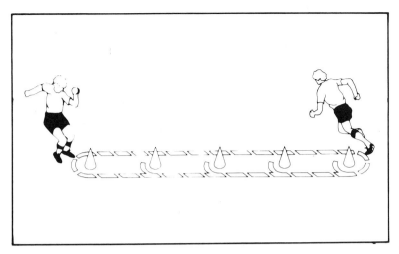

Diagram 1 The shuttle run. Place each of five cone markers five metres apart so that they are running in a straight line for 25 metres. The player must run to each marker, go round it and return to the starting point before setting off on a run to the next marker. He must race to and from each marker until taking a short rest before starting again.

must take turns to run to each marker, returning to the starting line after rounding the object and then immediately running round the next one until all five have been visited at sprint speed. A distance of 150 metres is covered on each run and the turns are the type you would get during a game. Make the players do five 'doggies' on the first day, six on the next and work up to a maximum of 15. Each player should make the run inside 45 seconds, with a 45 seconds rest period before starting on the next stint. *The fittest players are brought to their knees when they make 12 or more of these shuttle runs but once they have recovered from the exertion they will be confident they can face any amount of running in a match.* You can get the players to vary their times for the shuttle runs, alternating between stints of 30 seconds, 45 seconds and 60 seconds but stick to the same overall rest period.

For sprint work, you can have players racing each other from the halfway line to the goal-line but be careful not to continue this for too long a period or your speed work can develop into a test of endurance. Also work hard at the short sprints that are so vital to a footballer. Players should run as fast as they possibly can from the goal-line to the edge of the penalty area, then jog for 15 metres before finishing with a flat-out sprint to the half-way line.

The strength factor is important in the building of stamina and speed. Weight training can help develop vital power but this must be carried out only under specialist supervision. Among the exercises from which players can benefit, using weights worked out according to their size and strength, are:

SQUAT   Hold the weight behind the neck with the bar resting on the shoulders. Bend the knees to a squatting position and then rise again.

BENCH PRESS   Lie flat on your back with the bar resting beneath your chin.

25

Lift the weight to full arms stretch and then slowly bring it back to the starting position.

THE STEP-UP   Hold the weight firmly across the shoulders and step up on to a platform from 2 ft to 2 ft 6 in high.

The number of squats, presses and step-ups which are done depend on size and strength and should be worked out with a qualified trainer. Remember that this is weight training and not weight *lifting*. Too much weight work or training without proper supervision can lead to muscle strains. So be careful.

Training with the ball

The most important qualification for a player irrespective of his position is to be able to control the ball in any situation. It is a skill that comes naturally to some and is learned the hard way by others. But no matter how adept a player may be at controlling a ball he can only benefit and improve from practice, practice and yet more practice.

It is my personal belief that ball control is a vital area of our game that is too often neglected in British football. There are some professional players I could name who would not be able to trap a bag of cement. Too many players reach first-team status and then think: 'That's it. I'm here. I've arrived. I must be the completed article.' Consequently their game comes to a standstill at a time when they should be working during training at developing their ball skills.

It should be the duty and the desire of all professional footballers to gain complete command of the ball. They must be its master. Too often, even in the English First Division, you see players who are mastered by the ball. They are a disgrace to their profession.

My advice to any young player dreaming of being the next Pele, Bobby Charlton or George Best is that they must learn to love the ball and to achieve this they must live with it. It is vital to work with a ball during training. There used to be an old-fashioned idea that if you did not let your players touch a ball during mid-week training they'd be hungry for it by the time of the weekend match. This is nonsense.

To learn full control of the ball it must become second nature for a player to have it at his feet. He must cultivate a feel for the ball, learn to put the correct weight into it when giving measured passes and to know exactly how to bring it under instant control when receiving a pass.

Dribbling is a skill (sometimes a wasted skill) all of its own. What I am concerned with in this section on training with the ball is the pure basics. That is *receiving* the ball, *passing* it, *shooting* it, *heading* it and keeping *possession* of it.

Receiving the ball

If a player does not know how to *receive* a ball, there is little hope of him being able to pass it on for better use. Every player should learn the art of trapping the ball with his feet and also develop the ability to kill the ball with all parts of the body.

A prime example of what can be achieved by instant control came in the

1958 World Cup Final when the impeccable Pele — then 17 and a virtual unknown — took an awkward, swirling centre on his right thigh, flicked it across to his left, up on to his head and then swivelled round to volley an unstoppable shot past the Swedish goalkeeper.

This, of course, was a conjuror's control and beyond the ability of all but the greatest players. But I describe it to show what can be achieved. I believe all players should set their standards as high as possible. One of the things wrong with British football in recent years is that we have set our standards too low. We have been describing good passes as great and fair performances as good. So any player who thinks he knows all there is to know about receiving a ball should think of that Pele magic and ask himself if he can improve.

In training, the objective should be not only to improve a player's control but also to quicken it. The quicker a player can get command of the ball the more options he has open to him as to how to use it to the best advantages of the team.

What I recommend for training sessions is lots of group inter-passing. From distances of ten yards up to 30 yards, they should concentrate on passing the ball to each other as quickly and as accurately as possible. The players must get accustomed to receiving the ball at all angles and from all heights. They must master the 'quick kill' with the inside of the foot for balls coming at them at below knee height. These balls can be taken first of all standing still and then whilst running quickly. This type of control must be done without checking stride. Every player must work at perfecting a clean take of the ball and then moving it quickly on to a colleague.

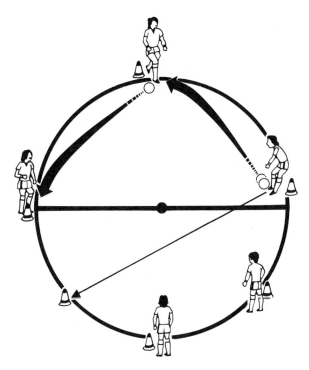

Diagram 2   Five players, with one ball and six cone markers, can sharpen their passing and receiving by working together in the centre-circle. Each player stands by a marker, leaving one marker unattended. The player in possession passes the ball to a colleague and then runs to the spare marker. The receiving player must pass the ball first time to a colleague and then run to the marker vacated by the first player. This process continues with the accent on one-touch play and with the player making the pass always running to the spare marker. To add to the difficulty of the routine, an extra player can be brought in to act as a piggy-in-the-middle defender. He changes places with the passing player if he intercepts the ball.

Trapping is a very necessary skill for all players. Balls coming out of the air can be controlled by using the inside or outside of the instep. A player should try to be properly balanced as the ball drops in front of him and he then gently traps it against the ground.

An important part of any training session when the *receiving* skills are put to the test are games of two-touch. These involve five- or six-a-side matches and the rule is that a player is allowed just two touches of the ball. One to control it and the second to pass or shoot. The ball must be played to the feet at all times and a free-kick is awarded against any player who kicks it above head height. This sort of competitive training is excellent for reflexes as well as instant control.

It is of course not always possible or even to a team's advantage to continually pass the ball along the ground. The *complete* player is able to receive and control a ball with all parts of his body. Training time should be given to catching the ball on the thigh, controlling it with the chest and the head.

Players should practise heading control in pairs. They can play two-touch, one to catch the ball on the forehead and two to head it back where the partner will go through the same process.

To simulate the pressures that a player would experience in a match, have balls chipped into a goalmouth where forwards and defenders can practise receiving the ball in confined space and with a challenge close at hand.

There is an old saying that it is better to give than to receive. In football it is vital to do both things well.

Diagram 3   Players can practise two-touch heading passes in pairs, one touch to control the ball and a second touch to head the ball to a colleague.

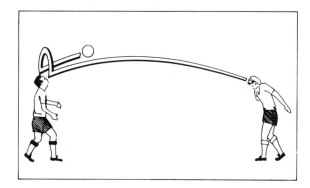

Passing the ball

I have stressed the absolute importance of *receiving* the ball. Now we come to the equally important technique of *giving* it. Time and again in all levels of football you see promising moves ruined by passes that are poorly placed or lacking in imagination.

There are many different variations of passes — short, long, chipped, curved, the through ball, the wall pass. All of them need to be practised and perfected during training.

Passing is all about accuracy and timing. A player must select the right player to pass to, the objective always being to give it to a colleague who is better positioned to achieve more with the ball.

Too often players pass simply because they are chickening out of the responsibility of holding the ball. They are the type who will get a colleague in trouble by passing to him when he is already tightly marked.

The good players who put the team before themselves look to use the ball to advantage at all times. Defenders should work in training at becoming masters of the long pass, practising at finding forward colleagues with 40 and 50 yard balls.

It is the midfield men who must be complete pass masters. They should be able to pass the ball accurately at any distance from ten to 50 yards and be adept at hitting curved passes that bend around the backs of defenders and long through passes that can split defences open down the middle.

Perhaps most of all they need judgment. The knowledge of knowing when to be inventive and imaginative and when to take the opportunity of providing a simple, direct pass that can be damaging to a defence. The midfield player who takes too long to distribute the ball or who tries to be clever when a simple pass needs to be delivered can stifle a team's progress. *The art of passing is not only about being accurate but is of giving the right ball at the right time.*

Wingers must of course perfect crosses, knowing exactly how weighted their pass must be to find the near post or the far post or wherever a striker might be waiting for service. They must also know when it is best to lay the ball back into the path of an oncoming colleague, rather than to cross it hopefully into a packed goalmouth where there could be a chance of losing possession.

Passing is not just about releasing the ball to a colleague. The best players know *where* the ball should be placed to produce the most problems for the opposition. It is about instinct, timing, accuracy, imagination and sometimes pure simplicity.

The receiver of course plays a crucial part in making the job easier for the man in possession by finding space ready for the delivery. This is achieved by intelligent running off the ball and getting into a position from where he can perform something positive once the pass has been made.

An effective method of beating a defence is with a wall pass. This calls for good understanding between two players and speed of thought and action on both their parts.

A perfect example of how it can work to devastating effect came when England played Wales at Wembley in 1969. Bobby Charlton was in possession and advancing at speed on the Welsh goal. The Welsh defenders positioned themselves to cancel out the chances of one of Bobby's famous sniper shots.

Bobby was a thought and a move ahead of them. He released a short pass to Francis Lee who cleverly gave a first-time return pass into Bobby's path. Suddenly the ball was no more than a blur as Bobby buried it deep into the Welsh net.

Lee had acted as the 'wall' for Charlton, returning the ball quickly and accurately. *The 'wall' man must not hesitate for a second. It must be an immediate return pass for the move to come off.*

It is very necessary to practise wall passes in training. This can be done in the five-a-side matches or by dividing the players up into teams of two-a-side and letting them try to outwit each other by using the wall-pass method.

The vital things for the two players to remember is that the man giving the

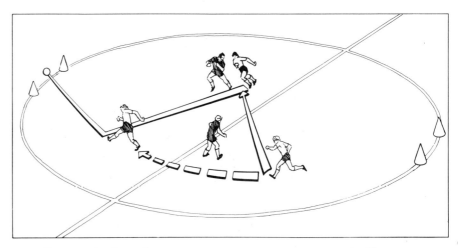

Diagram 4 Four players – two against two – can practice 'wall' passes in a confined area, such as the centre-circle. Set up miniature goals to introduce a competitive edge to the training. A goal can only be scored by a player on the receiving end of a return wall pass.

pass must run into space ready for the return and the receiver must release the ball instantly into the path of his team-mate.

It has to be done very quickly and the moment the man in possession feels it is 'on' he should shout to the player who is going to act as his wall. Players should be encouraged to call to each other during a match. A shout can alert a player to a situation that he has not appreciated.

Another useful pass that can be developed in training is the chip pass. It is imperative for a forward-going player to have this in his armoury if he finds himself confronted by a packed defence. He can cause confusion and chaos by dropping the ball like a mortar shell over their heads and into space behind them. The chip can be easily practised in training by breaking the players up into groups of three. One player acts as a sort of piggy in the middle, with one colleague facing him 15 yards away and the third player 15 yards behind

Diagram 5 The chip pass. The player in the centre (B) pushes the ball to the player facing him (A) and then rushes forward to put pressure on the receiving player who must chip the ball to the third player (C).

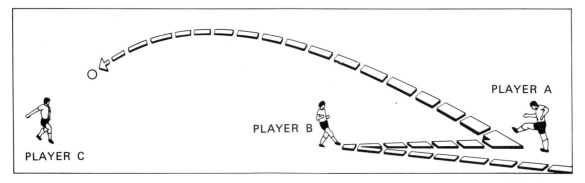

PLAYER C

PLAYER B

PLAYER A

him. The player in the middle pushes the ball to the man in front of him and then runs forward to put pressure on the receiver who must chip the ball to the third player. They then switch positions and start again.

It takes hours of practice to get the chip technique right but no self-respecting player should be without it. I am horrified to say that there are professional footballers in Britain who have not bothered to master the chip pass. That's like Jack Nicklaus going into a golf tournament without any short irons in his bag.

The chip pass can also be developed into a chip shot. A goalkeeper can get in useful practice by coming off his goal-line to narrow the angle as a team-mate attempts to chip the ball over his head. There is nothing quite as satisfying for a player than seeing his chip shot drop over the head of a goal-keeper and into the net. And there are few things more disconcerting for defenders than to have a pass chipped over their heads when they are grouping to cut out a ground pass.

The through pass remains one of the most telling passes in football. If it is struck correctly it can be like a dagger thrust to the heart of a defence. But anything less than accurate and it can give possession to the opposition.

It is not an easy pass to deliver but when there were players of the calibre of Johnny Haynes, John White, George Eastham, Bobby Charlton, Johnny Giles, Jimmy McIlroy and Bobby Collins around it was a real killer.

There was a time when the through ball almost became obsolete. Firstly because defenders had become all too aware of it and were able to cut it out and secondly because there was a sudden dearth of the sort of inside-forwards who could produce it to proper effect.

But with the emergence of players like Alan Hudson, Liam Brady, Don Masson, Tony Currie and Trevor Brooking the through ball was revived as a vital weapon in modern soccer.

The player delivering the through ball must disguise his intentions until the last moment while team-mates ahead of him jockey for position. *Ideally the ball should be played into space just ahead of the receiver so that he can shoot in his stride.* I have a painful memory of just how effective the tactic can be when Jimmy McCalliog's superbly placed through ball created the chance for Bobby Stokes to fire Southampton's winning goal against Manchester United in the 1976 FA Cup Final.

To practise it in training, three or four attacking players need to be marked by the same number of defenders with two midfield men lying deep and firing through balls into the penalty area from distances of 25 and 30 yards. The point to stress to players is that it takes two to make a pass successful, the giver and the receiver. It must be delivered with progress in mind. The receiver can help by getting himself into the best possible position to take charge of the ball.

An important part of any training session is the practising of passing variations. Whenever possible the password (if you'll excuse the pun) should be: *'Make it simple . . . make it quick.'*

The more the players practise inter-passing among themselves the easier it will be for them to find each other in match play. Have practice sessions with the forwards against the defenders, getting the players to concentrate on

Diagram 6   The goal that beat Manchester United in the 1976 FA Cup Final. Mike Channon plays a first-time pass to Jim McCalliog who strikes a perfect through ball behind the United defence. Southampton striker Bobby Stokes races on to the ball and fires a first-time shot beyond goalkeeper Alex Stepney and into the net.

Diagram 7   Running off the ball. In a two-against-two situation, Player B makes it easy for Player A to find him with a pass by intelligent running off the ball, leaving his marker standing.

passing quickly, accurately and with vision. Every forward should be running off the ball as if he is expecting the next pass to be made to him. This puts the defenders under pressure and gives the man in possession several options for his pass.

A player who is really thinking about his game will be looking for the opportunity to switch the direction of play. If you are in charge of a training session be sure to praise any player who is being imaginative as well as industrious. With the public and the Press, it is too often the goal scorer who gets all the credit when the ball goes into the net. The build-up is just as important as the end product because no forward can score unless the ball is coming through to him.

So remember to praise and encourage skilful and imaginative approach play in training. It will give players the confidence and incentive to do it in match situations.

I am a great believer in making training sessions as entertaining and as varied as possible. Too many coaches bore players with mundane methods and long lectures.

As far as I am concerned, training should be all about keeping players alert and interested and I go out of my way to praise a man who delivers a pass well because I know that with a little encouragement he will try to do it again when it really matters.

As I say, make it simple . . . make it quick. But find time in training to practise the unorthodox and the unusual.

An unpredictable pass that can throw a defence off guard is the back heel. It can be disconcerting for defenders but can also confuse colleagues unless it is well rehearsed in training.

I particularly remember a spectacular goal Denis Law scored when I recalled him to the Scotland team for the 1972 Home Championship. The match was against Northern Ireland at Hampden and the Irish were stubbornly holding us to a goalless draw until a combined moment of magic from Peter Lorimer and Law.

Lorimer was under pressure from goalkeeper Pat Jennings as he chased to intercept a poorly placed back pass from Pat Rice. It looked odds-on Jennings getting possession but Lorimer completely deceived him with a superb backheel with his right foot. Then he quickly turned and crossed the ball with his left to the six-yard line where Law scored with an acrobatic volley.

I describe this goal to illustrate what can be achieved with a back heel, particularly if it is a pass straight into the path of an oncoming colleague who can shoot while in full stride.

The back-heel is a relatively simple skill to master. What is harder to learn is the moments when it will prove of best advantage to the team. Forwards should take turns in using the back-heel technique in training, passing to a colleague while under pressure from a defender.

Another pass that should be perfected in training, particularly by the midfield players, is the swerved ball that bends around defenders and into the path of an attacking colleague.

Martin Peters provided a telling example of how a curled pass can dismantle a defence in the 1966 World Cup quarter-final match against Argentina at

Diagram 8 Martin Peters and Geoff Hurst combined for the England goal that beat Argentina in the 1966 World Cup quarter-finals. This diagram shows how Peters swerved the ball towards the near post where Hurst raced to meet it and to beat goalkeeper Roma with a glancing header.

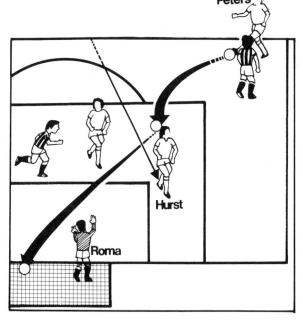

Wembley. He was in possession out on the left wing with a defender blocking his path to goal. Peters saw that Geoff Hurst was setting off on a diagonal run to the near post, a move perfected under Ron Greenwood's influence at West Ham. There seemed no way Peters could get the ball to his colleague but then he struck the ball with the outside of his left foot and sent it swerving around the defender in front of him to arrive at head height in time for Hurst to score with a delicate glancing header.

This was not something that just happened. Peters and Hurst had rehearsed it time and again while training with West Ham and their wonderful reward on this occasion was a place for England in the World Cup semi-finals.

A simple way to practise the 'big bender' is for the player in possession to position himself on one corner of the 18-yard line with a colleague making a diagonal run from the other corner. Once the two players are satisfied they have got the timing right and the angles right for the delivery of the swerved pass they should then polish it under pressure from two defenders.

Passing is a vital art for every member of the team. The more passing movements that are tried and tested in training the more variations will be available on match day when it really matters.

Shooting

Scoring goals is what football is all about, so accurate and powerful shooting is clearly of the utmost importance. Great goalscorers like Pele and Jimmy Greaves are born with their skill but any footballer can improve his finishing by prolonged practice.

Bobby Charlton has been one of the finest and deadliest finishers of modern football and I speak from chilling experience. I was marking Bobby when he made his debut for England against Scotland back in 1958 and was on the receiving end of one of the greatest goals ever scored at Hampden Park.

Tom Finney, then my Preston team-mate and just about the greatest thing on two feet, opened up our defence with a swerving run down the left before

34

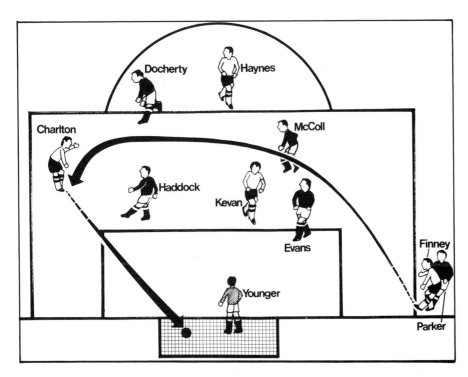

Diagram 9   This is a reconstruction of Bobby Charlton's first goal for
England in international football. Charlton leaves author Tommy
Docherty standing as he gives a perfect example of what can be achieved
by first-time shooting against Scotland at Hampden Park in 1958.

firing over a perfect centre. Bobby Charlton, showing the instinct and flair
that was to make him one of the world's most effective players, spurted away
from me and, as the ball came through at hip height, smashed it right footed
on the volley into the back of the net from 12 yards. Our great Scottish
goalkeeper Tommy Younger could only wave at the ball as it flashed past him.

It was the perfect example of what can be achieved by first-time shooting.
It was not just that the shot was right but Charlton's positioning and timing
which were spot-on. It was the sort of situation that all footballers become
familiar with in training but are rarely able to pull off in a match. It was a goal
that screamed the message: 'Practice makes perfect . . .'.

Players can practice in pairs, standing about 30 to 40 yards apart and
driving the ball as hard as possible at each other. They should be concentrating
on power, accuracy and striking the ball with *either* foot.

Shooting practice should not be confined to just the attacking players. *In
modern football, it is important that defenders should be able to take advantage of
any opening that presents itself for a shot at goal.*

You should involve all the players in shooting routines. One useful exercise
is to break them up into two groups. Group 'A' form a queue just off centre
and a couple of yards outside the penalty area. Group 'B' form a queue just
inside the by-line and about ten yards from the far post. The Group 'B' players

35

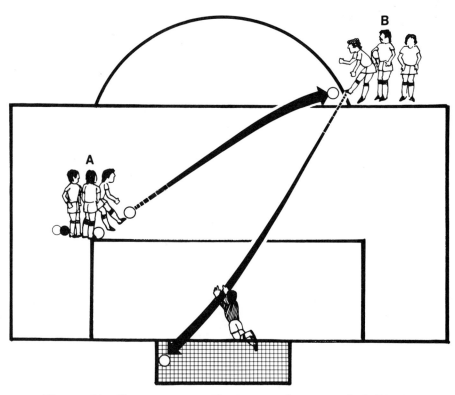

Diagram 10 Shooting practice. The Group A players pass the ball back
into the path of the Group B players who take turns to shoot for goal.

each have a ball and take it in turns to play it back into the path of a team-
mate from Group 'A' who must shoot first time and try to beat the goalkeeper.

When all the Group 'A' players have had three shots each, they then switch
positions with the Group 'B' players and provide them with a ball service. The
balls should be played back at varying heights and speeds so that the players
can practice shots on the volley, the half volley and lob and ground shots.

A fun way of improving the volleying technique of players is to organise
games of three and four-a-side volley tennis. This is played on a tennis court
space with a net in the middle, with the scoring rules the same as in lawn
tennis. The players can volley the ball back over the net or kick it back on the
half volley. A player can use his body — chest, thighs, head or feet — to keep
possession of the ball before kicking it back provided he does not let it bounce
twice.

Players must practice at shooting when in full stride with a moving ball and
also take plenty of shots with a stationary ball.

To improvise match situations, have the wingers crossing high and low
balls into the goalmouth with the forwards briefed to shoot first time under
pressure from defenders.

This will sharpen their reactions in the six-yard box where games are won
and lost depending on the speed and opportunism of the forwards. To get the
players really alert, have one-touch five-a-side matches when first-time

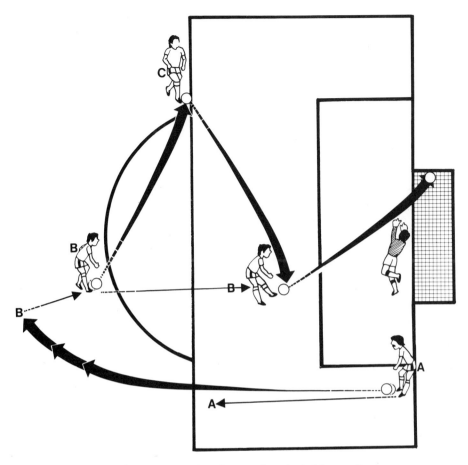

Caption 11 This is one routine that can be adapted for continuous shooting practice. One player passes the ball from the bye-line to a colleague running towards goal from a distance of 25 to 30 yards. The receiver controls the ball while in full stride, fetches it forward and then plays a one-two with a third man before shooting. He goes to the bye-line and sends a pass into the path of the first player who has run into a receiving position about 15 yards outside the penalty area. They continually repeat this move, testing the goalkeeper with chips and lobs as well as first-time shots.

passing and first-time shooting is a must otherwise they lose possession to the opposition.

For long-range shots, players should practice playing one-two passes with each other 25 to 35 yards from goal and then one of them unleashing a shot. Defenders in particular should be encouraged to take part in this routine so that they can rifle in 'sniper' shots when the opportunity is there in match situations.

Shooting of course is not only about blasting the ball at full power. Make sure that your training sessions include the practice of chip shots, lobs, swerved shots and the improvement of accuracy from close range.

Heading

A footballer is not complete until he has learnt how to use his head, both from a thinking and a physical point of view. There are three main functions when heading a ball – the headed clearance, headed goal and headed pass. Each of them is equally important and matches can be decided by a team's strength or weakness in the air.

A headed clearance from in front of goal should, ideally, be directed to a team-mate. But this is not always possible when the pressure is on, in which case the defender heading the ball should concentrate on getting height and distance. His objective must be to get the ball as far as possible away from the goal area and preferably towards the touchline. This will give his colleagues time to regroup and reorganize and to pick up any opponents who are not properly marked.

This clearance technique, particularly the responsibility of the two centre-backs, can be performed in training by having the wingers sending over a stream of high crosses that are to be cleared while the forwards are challenging.

At the same time, of course, the forwards can practice heading at goal. While the defenders will be trying to head the ball *up* and away it will be the aim of the forwards to head the ball *down*, either into the net or as a pass to the feet of a colleague.

Heading skill is all about timing, spring, positioning and power. The higher a player can jump the more command he will have in the goal area. Neck muscles can be developed with specialized weight training under expert

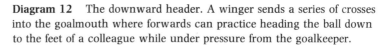

Diagram 12   The downward header. A winger sends a series of crosses into the goalmouth where forwards can practice heading the ball down to the feet of a colleague while under pressure from the goalkeeper.

Spring in the air...Stuart Pearson (left) and Jimmy Case show the elevation top players get when heading the ball. Heading skill is all about timing, spring, positioning and power.

coaching and the timing of runs and heading with a jack-knife action can be perfected by constant practice.

I find footballers always enjoy and benefit from games of head tennis, similar to volley tennis but the net is higher and only the head is allowed to be used. It helps the players develop control and timing.

Back headers from the near post at corners and other deadball situations are always a useful tactic to have and should be regularly practised in training.

No matter how the game evolves tactically, there will always be a place in the game for the far-post ball that will call for heading power from forwards and defenders alike.

Ideally, the far-post ball — the main weapon of wingers — should be aimed just out of reach of the goalkeeper. The best place for the forward to direct his header is down and across the goal because the goalkeeper will almost certainly be scrambling to cover the post nearest to where the ball has been driven by the winger.

This must be performed time and again in training as very necessary practice for the goalkeeper and defenders as well as the forwards. Time must also

39

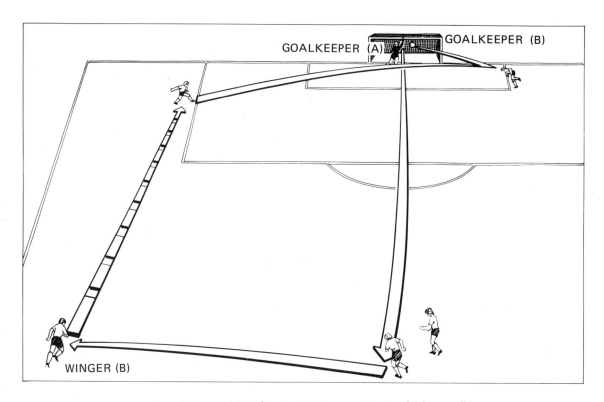

GOALKEEPER (A)   GOALKEEPER (B)

WINGER (B)

Diagram 13   This is a training routine in which a goalkeeper can practice his throwing technique and the forwards can work at headers at the near and far post. The goalkeeper throws the ball out to a defender who plays it into the path of a winger. He takes the ball forward before crossing it to the far post. The move is then repeated, this time with the winger dropping the ball to the near post. Full-backs should sometimes do the winger's job so that they can perfect a finish to their overlapping play.

be given to dropping the ball short to the near post where attackers should be looking for the chance to put the ball into the net with glancing headers.

Heading, like so much in football, is about an attitude of mind. A player must make up his mind that he wants the ball . . . that he must win it . . . and then go for it with confidence and determination.

As an example of what can be achieved by intelligent headwork, I am almost invariably reminded of Pele in the 1970 World Cup Final against Italy. He laid on the third goal for Jairzinho with a header that I am convinced 999 out of a thousand players would not have dreamt of making. It was so simple yet so stunningly effective. Gerson, as accurate with his left foot as Nicklaus is with a '9' iron, sent the ball arcing over the Italian defence to Pele who was loitering with intent just beyond the far post.

Pele had three choices as the ball came to him head high. He could head for goal, bring the ball under control and shoot or pass the ball on. Most players I am sure would have elected to have a go at goal themselves but Pele, with his great vision, had seen a situation that had escaped most eyes.

He calmly headed the ball down into the path of Jairzinho to completely confuse an Italian defence that was bracing itself for a goal assault from Pele. The manoeuvre was so stunning in its simplicity that Jairzinho had time to ram the ball into the net after miskicking at his first attempt.

The goal had been made by a piece of sheer Pele magic that went unheralded by many people who just did not appreciate the subtlety of what he had done.

Pele had demonstrated exactly what I mean by using your head at football!

Keeping possession

Football is basically a simple game, often made more complicated than it need be by the people who play it and the people who teach it. The one fact to bear in mind is that to score goals a team must be in possession of the ball. In football, possession is not just 99 per cent but *all* of the law.

The way a team keeps possession once it has the ball is by intelligent passing, positioning and generalship. Dribbling is one way for a player to retain the ball while his team-mates look for space where they can receive it. But the player who dribbles for the sake of it can anchor a team's progress and must be disciplined into making an earlier release of the ball.

Nevertheless, dribbling is an art that performed properly and at the right time can have a devastating effect on a match. A simple routine for practising dribbling is to have a dozen players, all with balls at their feet, moving quickly

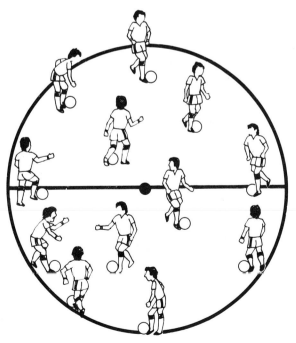

Diagram 14   This routine will test the close control of players when working at speed in a confined and crowded space. Each of 12 players has a ball. They move about at speed in the centre-circle, keeping close control of the ball and avoiding contact with each other.

around the centre-circle. Their concentration should be on keeping close control of the ball and avoiding each other.

An important factor for a player attempting to beat defenders by dribbling is to have a change of pace. There are many footballers, even in the English First Division, who have sound ball control but are unable to penetrate defences simply because they lack acceleration and are one paced, and are therefore predictable and easy to shut out.

A cardinal sin that even top players commit is to dribble without knowing what is happening around them. The true artists are always aware of what is going on off the ball and plan accordingly,

Players can sharpen their skills by playing five- and six-a-side matches in which they must beat an opponent before passing the ball.

Another training routine using just the centre circle involves five players. Three try to retain possession of the ball while the other two continually challenge and harrass them. In such a small space, ball control has to be really tight and the passing short, quick and accurate.

When one of the two defenders succeeds in intercepting the ball he changes place with the one who last kicked it. Always keep it to three against two.

It is often necessary to play patient, possession football against a negative, defensive side. The objective is gradually to draw them out of defence and then strike quickly forward the moment a gap appears.

This demands good ball control and a tactical awareness by all the players. Everybody should be looking to make supporting runs and this tactic can be developed in training by playing six forwards against five defenders and a

Diagram 15 Another simple routine for improving support play. In an area about 15 yards square, three men try to keep possession while being harrassed by one player. Provided the pass is made early enough and the two supporting players run off the ball with intelligence possession should not be lost. After five minutes, the defending player changes places with one of his three colleagues and the routine of keeping possession starts again.

goalkeeper. *Stress to the players that it is the men off the ball who determine how long their side can keep possession by taking up the best possible positions to receive the ball.*

England's success in the 1966 World Cup was largely due to what their players achieved off the ball.

Geoff Hurst and Roger Hunt were both unselfish and full of stamina and ready to run marathon distances with or without the ball. Both these players showed what can be achieved by proper training, planning and organization.

Tackling

It's a simple fact that to gain possession of the ball you have to win it. Tackling remains one of the most effective ways of taking the ball from an opponent.

There are six golden rules for a tackling player to remember:

1) Keep your eye on the ball all the time.
2) Never tackle from out of range.
3) Tackle whenever possible with the full weight of the body.
4) The leading foot in the tackle should be aimed at the centre of the ball.
5) Always try to keep goal-side of the player in possession.
6) Never tackle unless there is at least a 50-50 chance of winning the ball except in extreme circumstances.

The great tacklers of football aim at not only dispossessing their opponents but at being in full control of the ball when they come out of the tackle.

For a descriptive account of the perfect tackle, I turn once again to the 1970 World Cup. I was in Guadalajara for England's match against Brazil and vividly recall a moment when Bobby Moore revealed his very real talent as a defender.

It was early in the second-half and the highly-skilled Jairzinho was in possession and racing towards the England goal in a mood to cause disruption. Just Moore stood between him and a quick route to goal. It looked ominous for England because the Brazilian right winger had proved time and again that in these man-to-man situations he was one of the Great Untouchables.

Moore bided his time and then suddenly moved forward to meet Jairzinho with an upright, determined challenge. He blocked the ball with his right foot and came striding powerfully out of the tackle in possession as Jairzinho tumbled off balance under the weight of the challenge.

It was a masterly exhibition of tackling. Everything was right. Moore waited for the right moment to commit himself. He was always goalside. He was correctly balanced when he made his challenge and he came out with the ball at his feet. It was the perfect block tackle.

All players, not just defenders, should know the fundamental principles of tackling. In training, let them practice in pairs with player 'A' trying to take the ball past player 'B' who must attempt to stop him with a tackle. Then reverse the roles.

A tackle that is sometimes necessary as a last resort is the sliding tackle. The timing is all important and it requires considerable practice. This tackle is launched at speed from a distance, the tackler sliding in from an angle to win the ball with an outstretched leg.

It can again be practised in pairs, with player 'A' running towards goal for

Diagram 16   The tackle. The tackler must keep his eye on the ball all the time, getting close to the man in possession and picking the right moment to challenge when he knows he can get the whole weight of his body behind the tackle (Fig. 1). The tackling foot should be aimed at the centre of the ball, with the knee turned outwards and the ankle held firm (Fig. 2).

a shot while player 'B' launches a sliding tackle at an angle from a distance of about six yards.

The most important factor in tackling is timing. The secret is not only of knowing how to tackle but when.

Ideally, the tackle should be made immediately the player receives the ball and before he has had time to bring it under proper control. But this is rarely possible and in modern football it is imperative that a defender must not commit himself to a tackle unless he is convinced he is going to win the ball.

Defenders must learn to hold off and jockey the player in possession into a position where he can do least damage, tackling only when he knows he can

The mis-timed tackle... Mike Channon has made this Italian defender tackle from out of range in a desperate bid to stop the England striker's advance on goal. The great tacklers of football aim at not only dispossessing their opponents but at being in full control of the ball when they come out of the tackle.

come out with the ball. The *thinking* defender will always position himself to try to win the ball by interception rather than the more risky tackle.

Practice marking, tackling, covering and jockeying in training by playing four against six outside the penalty area. The four attacking players must try to fetch the ball into the penalty box while the six defenders will concentrate on tackling the player in possession, marking tightly and covering for each other.

Play six-a-side matches on a half-size pitch, the player in possession having to dribble past an opponent before passing. The opponent can only win the ball for his side by making a winning tackle.

Goalkeeping

The goalkeeper requires specialist training, as often as possible in the company of the back four defenders with whom he will be needing a close rapport and understanding for critical match situations.

Here is how training methods can help a goalkeeper develop his game:

HANDLING   The two or three goalkeepers in your squad should practice together. They can warm up by throwing the ball to each other at differing heights and speeds, concentrating on catching the ball cleanly.

Gradually increase the pace and alter the trajectory of the throws until each of the goalkeepers is having to leap in all directions to catch the ball. To put a

45

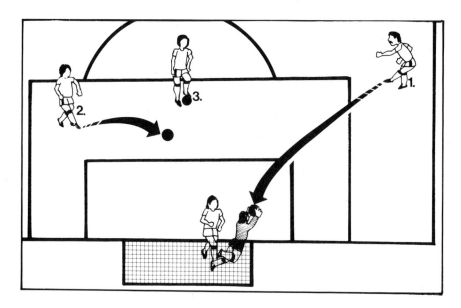

Diagram 17   Pressure training for the goalkeeper. Three forwards each have a ball and a fourth has the job of continually harrassing the goalkeeper. The three players with the balls take turns in shooting at goal. It is all done at high speed and the second the goalkeeper has gathered the ball or it has gone into the net, he must position himself to face the next shot. The players can also test him with crosses and lob shots.

bit of spark and competitiveness into this routine, points can be awarded for clean catches, the first to reach 25 being awarded the goalkeeper's yellow jersey for the rest of the training session.

The goalkeepers should have a period when they are mixing their handling practice with improving their throwing accuracy. They can stand some 25 to 35 yards apart, hurling the ball one-handed to each other.

An exercise that will help reactions as well as improve handling is to have four or five outfield players taking alternate shots at speed from the edge of the penalty area. As the goalkeeper catches the ball he must toss it to one side and concentrate on stopping the next shot. Build up the speed of this routine until shots are raining in on the goalkeeper.

The wingers can help a goalkeeper develop the art of cutting out crosses by firing over a stream of high centres from either wing. To simulate match situations two forwards should put the goalkeeper under pressure as he attempts to catch the crosses.

Crucial points for any goalkeeper to remember are:
● He must always keep his eye on the ball.
● Whenever possible, get the body behind the ball as a second barrier when making a save.
● If taking an overhead catch, bring the ball down to the chest at the first opportunity.

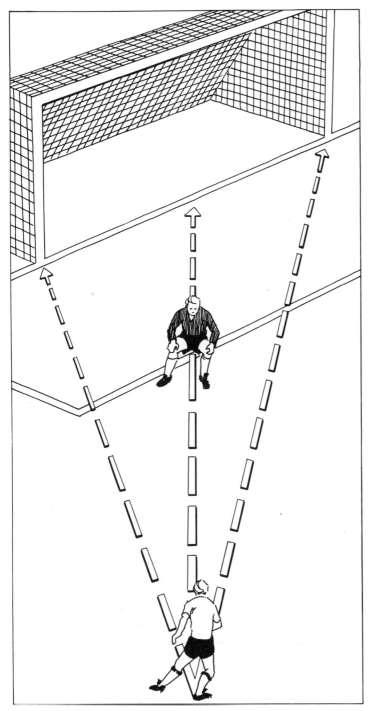

Diagram 18 The goalkeeper must come out to narrow the angle, moving towards the tip of an imaginary triangle. He must be positioned on the 'bisector' line of the triangle.

● Always be positive because a hesitant goalkeeper can drain the confidence of an entire defence.

There are times when it is hazardous for a goalkeeper to attempt to catch a ball. In training, he should give a lot of time and practice to fisting the ball away, using one and two fists to direct the ball as far away from the goalmouth as possible.

It is vital to have all the defenders and the goalkeeper working in unison and this can only be achieved by them continually working together in training, practising as much as possible under improvized match conditions.

POSITIONING   The efficient goalkeeper who has really studied his game knows how to make his job easier by being in the right place at the right time. *The secret of sound goalkeeping is safe handling allied with good positional sense.*

Too many goalkeepers scramble through matches, relying on their instinct and reflexes to get them out of trouble. It is imperative that he should know exactly when to leave his goal-line. There are two main reasons for coming off the line: to get the ball and/or to narrow the angle so as to shrink the target area for an approaching attacker.

Positioning, particularly for the experienced goalkeeper, is part instinctive but if he has done his homework properly he will know just how far he has to advance off his line to prevent an attacker from beating him with a shot. He must make a study of angles so that when he comes off the goal-line he knows exactly how much space is left either side of him in relation to the two goalposts. Ideally, he should be in a central position at the tip of an imaginary triangle so that he has equal space either side of him. Or he can knowingly leave a wider space on one side in an attempt to persuade the attacker where to place his shot.

Goalkeeping is about geometry and geography. The reliable goalkeeper knows his angles and also every inch of the penalty area. He has to know

Diagram 19   A simple training routine to help goalkeepers perfect their timing for coming off the goal-line. Balls are directed to the front section of the penalty area and the goalkeeper must try to gather each ball before an advancing forward gets to it.

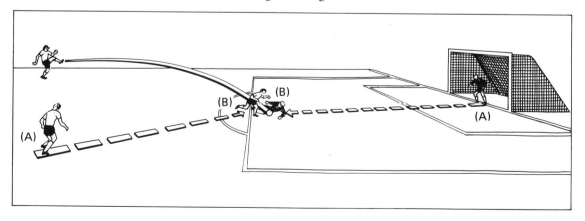

where he is at all times and by intelligent positioning and thoughtful patrolling of the penalty area he can become almost an all-purposes 'sweeper' at the back of the defence.

He must practise his positioning during every training session, particularly in the five- and six-a-side matches and also when going through his catching routines. Everytime he collects the ball he must check his positioning until he can get around the goal area blind folded.

Forwards can help him in training by advancing on the goal with the ball at their feet. He must come off his line and narrow the angle for their shots. In these situations, the goalkeeper can also practice the technique of whipping the ball off the attacker's toes. It demands courage, expert timing and safe handling to perform it properly. But the goalkeeper will consider the practice well worth while when he pulls it off during a moment of pressure in a match.

A tip here. Every team must have a second-choice goalkeeper, an outfield player who can double in goal in emergency. Ensure that the second-choice man gets plenty of practice between the posts, preferably in the company of a specialist goalkeeper who can advise him on all aspects of guarding the goal.

DISTRIBUTION   A goalkeeper should work at being able to use a ball with the same amount of accuracy, imagination and distance as any outfield player.

The second the ball is in his hands or at his feet he should be thinking in terms of putting the foundations to a counter attack by distributing it with progress in mind.

Uppermost in his mind should be two thoughts:
● How to use the ball to the team's advantage.
● How to use it with a minimum risk of losing possession.

Too many goalkeepers turn distribution into a lottery. They blindly belt the ball down the middle of the field where, often as not, their forwards are out-numbered which straightaway puts the odds on the opposition gaining possession.

Ideally, a goalkeeper should be looking to give the ball to an unmarked colleague who has time and space to control it without coming under instant pressure from an opponent.

This calls for thought and action from the outfield players as well as the goalkeeper. He should practice in training, particularly with his two full-backs, the short, rolled pass with one hand that can trigger a counter attack from deep in defence. For this to work to the best advantage, it is important that the ball should be rolled into the path of the receiving defender who must be running in anticipation of the ball coming to him.

The ball can be rolled underarm or thrown overarm, depending on the power and the distance needed. The goalkeeper should also practice at long distance throwing, working hard at it until he is as accurate as a top-class cricket fielder is at putting the ball over the top of the stumps from the boundary.

It helps a goalkeeper in moments of crisis if he can clear a ball with either foot because the opposition can quickly put the pressure on a one-footed kicker by the simple tactic of having a player stand close to his kicking side.

As well as deadball kicking, the goalkeeper should give plenty of practise to the volley and half-volley from the hands. The drop-kick is an important weapon in his armoury because the lower trajectory will carry the ball much farther, especially when it is being kicked into a strong head wind.

Diagram 20 The goalkeeper practises receiving pass backs from a defensive colleague (1) and then throws it to the feet of another defender (2). He passes the ball back to the goalkeeper who throws it to the first defender and so on.

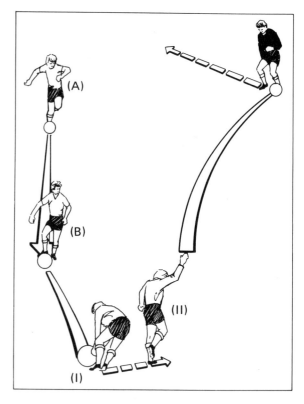

The goalkeeper should practise all his short-clearance methods in the company of the back four defenders, and the midfield men and forwards should take part when he is going for distance clearances so that in match situations they know just where he is likely to drop the ball for them to take possession.

COMMAND   An entire defence can be inspired by the confidence of a goalkeeper. He must be the complete commander of his area, shouting positional instructions and leaving his own defenders and the opposing forwards in no doubt that he is the master.

There are three 'Bs' for goalkeepers:

● Be positive.
● Be the boss.
● Be first.

Hesitation can be fatal for a goalkeeper. The dithering goalkeeper can wreck the confidence of a team. He must *be first* to decide whose ball it is going to be when it is approaching the danger area.

If he makes up his mind that it is going to be his, he should let everybody know by calling 'Mine' and then go for it with determination. If he believes a colleague is better positioned to deal with it he should be equally positive and shout 'Yours'.

The goalkeeper's complete command must be ascertained in training with the defenders drilled into accepting he is in charge of the goal area. They must get used to shouting to each other, giving and receiving orders that are brief and easy to understand in the heat of battle.

50

PENALTIES   Saving penalties is often as much about gambling as goalkeeping. The man on the goal-line must make up his mind which way he thinks the penalty taker is going to place the ball and dive hoping he has picked the right direction.

At the top level, the goalkeepers make a study of all the penalty experts in their division and make mental notes of which way they like to place the ball and whether they concentrate on direction or power.

A goalkeeper can practise trying to save penalties in training by having his team-mates taking turns at firing the ball from the 12-yard spot.

The odds are always in favour of the man taking the penalty but the astute goalkeeper can cut the odds by once again being *positive* on the goal-line. If he is a good enough actor, he can by just looking and leaning his body slightly to one side persuade the penalty taker that he knows which side he is about to place the ball and at the same time be mentally prepared to dive *the other* way.

It is all about a battle of wits and there are times when a goalkeeper can out-fox a penalty taker who is perhaps lacking confidence in his own ability. He has a big target to aim at but it can shrink considerably if the goalkeeper facing him exudes confidence.

Goalkeeping is one of the most difficult jobs in football. The best motto for goalkeepers to adopt is: Safety first. Spectators are often deceived by a goal-keeper, thinking he is better than he is because he performs saves that are spectacular. Many times he is having to be spectacular because his positioning

Safe as the Banks of England…Gordon Banks in classical action as he makes a flying save from a Kevin Hector shot. Banks was a master of positional play and always had a total awareness of where he needed to be to make his work that much easier.

It's my ball!...Peter Shilton shows the confident handling that has made him one of the world's outstanding goalkeepers. Shilton plays with an assurance that has a calming influence on the players around him even when the pressure is at its peak.

A knockout punch...Alex Stepney fists the ball away during the 1977 FA Cup Final between Manchester United and Liverpool. Ideally, a goalkeeper should try to catch the ball but if under the sort of pressure being applied here by Ray Kennedy then a fisted clearance is the next best thing.

is wrong. The goalkeeper who has done his homework can make a difficult save look easy simply by knowing where to be at the right time.

Almost inevitably I am drawn again to that Brazil-England match in Mexico during the 1970 World Cup for an example of what can be achieved by a goalkeeper who has made a complete study of his job.

Jairzinho accelerated beyond Terry Cooper to the byline in a right wing raid in the 10th minute of that memorable match. He aimed a centre towards the far post, some seven or eight yards out. Pele positioned himself expertly to receive the ball and rose majestically to get above and behind the ball in a classic exhibition of how to perform a header.

He arched his back and neck for full power and drove his header down towards the goal-line for what seemed a certain goal. Gordon Banks had been stationed at the near post to cover Jairzinho's cross and seemed hopelessly positioned. But then in a sudden blur of movement he hurled himself back across his goal and as Pele's header struck the ground two feet from the goal-line he stretched himself to send the ball miraculously over the crossbar with an upward flicking movement of his right hand.

It was the greatest save I have ever seen and to this day even Pele wonders how he managed it.

You could not teach anybody to make a save like this. But you can train them so that their reactions, thoughts, movements and reflexes are considerably quickened.

All goalkeepers should think of what Gordon Banks achieved against Pele and so realize that in football all things are possible.

The next move…The instant Liverpool goalkeeper Ray Clemence
has taken possession you can see he is looking where to place it in
the best interests of his team. Clemence is a master of intelligent
distribution.

The high and the mighty…Goalkeepers must get good elevation as
demonstrated here by West Germany's ace-in-the-air Sepp Maier
during the 1970 World Cup quarter-final match against England. He
has timed his jump to perfection while England attackers Geoff Hurst
(centre) and Martin Peters are unable to make a positive challenge.

3

Strategy

There is so much mumbo jumbo talked about the strategy of football that I am surprised some coaches don't disappear with a flash and a bang when they are talking to their confused players.

For me, strategy in football is all about *planning*. It is to do with working to the strengths and disguising the weaknesses of the players you have available, finding the system of play that suits them best and making them aware of the positive contribution they can make within the framework of the selected team formation.

Strategy for too many coaches can be interpreted as meaning 'straitjacket'. They stifle the thoughts and actions of their players by putting too many barriers in their way.

A predecessor of mine as manager of the Scottish international team once instructed Eddie McCreadie, then a thrusting and intuitive left-back, to ration himself to exactly three overlapping runs during a crucial match.

Now how can a player give any sort of a natural performance when anchored by orders as stupid and as blinkered as that? Players must be given a certain amount of freedom otherwise you are going to produce a team of robots who will fall apart the moment the unexpected happens. And football is full of the unexpected which makes it the gripping, exciting game that it is.

In this chapter, I propose to give a complete breakdown of soccer strategy as I see it with a study of overall team organization and the responsibilities of the individual players who have to make it work.

But first of all I must stress that in my opinion no system should be enforced so rigidly that the progress of players is stifled. Work at making players adaptable and intelligent in a soccer sense so that they know just when to be inventive and when to introduce variety into their game.

Playing formations

When I first came into professional football with Glasgow Celtic back in 1949 the playing system employed by most clubs was based on the third-back game introduced at Arsenal by the legendary Herbert Chapman in the late 1920s.

This revolved around the centre-half, an attack-oriented player in the early days of football, dropping back into a deep central defensive position with the two full-backs playing level with him but wide on the flanks to mark the wingers.

The full-backs swivelled or pivoted on the centre-half who was always positioned in the middle as the linchpin of the defence. If play was concentrated down the left, then the right-back would swing around into a position where he could counter any attempted breakthrough.

The two wing-halves — my role was as a right-half — were on patrol in the middle of the field with orders to pick up their rival inside-forwards and prompt the forward line with a supply of passes.

In this system, the five forwards lined up in a W-formation. Two ball-playing inside-forwards patrolled just behind the three front men, with the two wingers wide near the touchlines and the centre-forward carrying a lot of responsibility down the middle. This is how the formation looked:

GOALKEEPER

RIGHT-BACK   LEFT-BACK
CENTRE-HALF

RIGHT-HALF   LEFT-HALF

INSIDE-RIGHT   INSIDE-LEFT

OUTSIDE-RIGHT   CENTRE-FORWARD   OUTSIDE-LEFT

Early in my career with Celtic I was lucky to come under the influence of a little, white-haired Englishman called Jimmy Hogan who was coaching at the club after a spell as Scotland's advisor.

It was Hogan who first opened my eyes to the possibilities of sweeping tactical changes in British football. He was a perceptive man with great vision but, incredibly, the established stars would have nothing to do with him at Celtic. They dismissed his theories as total rubbish.

Yet it was this same Jimmy Hogan, as a coach first in Austria and then Hungary, who helped lay the seeds of the great football tactical revolution that was finally to embrace Britain. I have heard Sir Matt Busby referred to as the Father of Football. Jimmy Hogan deserves a share of that title.

There was a tactical standstill in Britain in the years immediately after the Second World War and it was not until the Hungarians shattered England 6-3 at Wembley and then 7-1 in Budapest that people started to realize how far we had slipped behind the rest of the world.

I twice played against those magical Magyars in 1955–56 and rate them one of the greatest international teams of all time. I shall take a wide-ranging look at their special skills and style in the chapter on outstanding international sides but suffice to say they opened the eyes of all *thinking* British footballers to what could be achieved by movement off the ball, support running and the adaptation of traditional positional play.

Scotland were beaten both times by the Hungarians, 4-2 at Hampden Park and 3-1 in Budapest. But even in defeat I would willingly have paid for the experience of playing against them.

What impressed me most was the speed with which they switched defence to attack, using right-half Boszik and withdrawn centre-forward Hidegkuti as link men who quickly transferred the ball to flying wingers Budai and Czibor who then continued the conveyor belt of passes by getting the ball to the artistic Kocsis or on to the ferocious left foot of the untouchable Puskas.

The deep-lying centre-forward strategy of Hidegkuti was copied with some success by Don Revie at Manchester City as British clubs slowly but surely realized that changes in our conventional game were vital if we were not to become completely stagnant.

Football moved into the modern era in 1958 when Brazil magically won the World Cup in Sweden playing to a revolutionary 4-2-4 formation. This is how that magnificent team lined up, with the stunning 17-year-old Pele making his debut on the world stage:

GOALKEEPER
(Gylmar)

	RIGHT-	LEFT-	
RIGHT-BACK	CENTREBACK	CENTREBACK	LEFT-BACK
(D. Santos)	(Bellini)	(Orlando)	(N. Santos)

LINK-MAN   LINK-MAN
(Zito)   (Didi)

OUTSIDE-RIGHT	STRIKER	STRIKER	OUTSIDE-LEFT
(Garrincha)	(Vava)	(Pele)	(Zagalo)

It was an attractive style of play that was imitated by many teams throughout the world. In defence, the two central defenders provided cover for each other and the full-backs started to position themselves alongside opposing wingers, cramping their style and stopping them from receiving the ball in space.

The way Brazil played it, the six front men were all attack conscious. Zito and the deadly Didi were constructive and inventive midfield link-men providing a highly skilled service for the four marvellously talented front runners, with Garrincha and Zagalo often cutting in from the wings to add their striking power to the unstoppable tandem team of Vava and Pele.

The 4-2-4 system worked for Brazil simply because they had the players with the technical ability to make it work. In fact that Brazilian team was so talented they could probably have won the 1958 World Cup if they had decided to play in one line!

But so many of the teams that switched to 4-2-4 disappeared in a maze of their own making because they did not have the players equipped to make the system work smoothly.

The success of any system depends on the quality of the players available. Coaches and managers would be well advised to fit a system to their players not their players to a system. Play to your strengths and disguise your weaknesses.

Not all the countries followed Brazil's 4-2-4 formation. The Italians

Rodney Marsh...a skilful individualist who had great flair and style. But his inventive play was not always appreciated by his Manchester City team-mates. Gifted players like Marsh have to be fitted into the framework of the team but without having their natural skill stifled.

persevered with and perfected a system that very nearly succeeded in strangling the life right out of their football.

Famous coaches like Nereo Rocco and Helenio Herrera became trapped by the fear of defeat and encouraged the growth of a stifling system called *catenaccio*.

It means 'chain' or 'bolt' defence and was originally the brainchild of an Austrian coach, Karl Rappan, who introduced it when in charge of the Swiss national team.

Catenaccio is totally defensive and negative, with its chief feature being that it employs a 'sweeper' operating behind a line of four backs. His job is to cover for any defender who may be under pressure and to quickly plug any gaps that may appear in the defensive wall.

I personally am not a great lover of this system. It is not progressive or positive enough for my liking but I recognize that there are occasions when its operation can sometimes produce a result that would be beyond a team playing a more adventurous game.

I have seen *catenaccio* teams playing in Italy with three midfield men and only two strikers. To me, this is coward's football and an insult to the spectators who have paid to see some entertainment.

The more commonly employed *catenaccio* system is a little more adventurous, with two creative link-men in midfield providing passes for three front runners. This is how this formation looks:

GOALKEEPER

SWEEPER

RIGHT-   LEFT-
RIGHT-BACK   CENTREBACK   CENTREBACK   LEFT-BACK

LINK-MAN   LINK-MAN

STRIKER   STRIKER   STRIKER

Feyenoord of Holland gave an exhilarating exhibition of how *catenaccio* can be used as a springboard for attack when they beat Celtic in the 1970 European Cup Final. They frustrated and contained Celtic by using conventional *catenaccio* tactics in the first-half and then unleashed a series of brilliant counter attacks that cracked Celtic after half-time. Hasil and Van Hanegem took command of the midfield and the powerful Israel was released from a disciplined sweeper role to move forward and add extra weight and dimension to the Feyenoord attack. Celtic were driven back into desperate defence and were finally beaten by goals from Israel and Kindvall after leading 1-0 from a thundering Tommy Gemmell free-kick.

It was an object lesson for all coaches that formations should be kept flexible, with the players improvizing and using their imagination.

British football had meantime moved on (or back) from a mass move towards 4-2-4 formations to the 4-3-3 line-up that proved so successful for

Alf Ramsey's England team in the 1966 World Cup.

Alf was given the credit for developing this strategy but I recall that in the 1958 World Cup Final against Sweden Brazil pulled left winger Zagalo — manager of the 1970 World Cup winners — back in the first-half to play a withdrawn role in a 4-3-3 line-up.

Alf's use of the system proved the value of shaping a formation to the strength of the players available. He began to experiment on a new theme at Ipswich when he had veteran Jimmy Leadbetter, wearing a No. 11 shirt, stationed in midfield and made him the chief provider of passes for twin strikers Ted Phillips and Ray Crawford and fast, orthodox right winger Roy Stephenson.

Ipswich, superbly organized, won the League championship in 1962 just a couple of months before Brazil retained the World Cup in Chile playing a flexible 4-3-3.

Moving on to the England manager's job, Alf gave birth to the 'wingless wonders' and captured the World Cup in 1966 with this line-up:

GOALKEEPER
(Banks)

RIGHT-BACK   RIGHT-CENTREBACK   LEFT-CENTREBACK   LEFT-BACK
(Cohen)   (Jack Charlton)   (Moore)   (Wilson)

DEFENSIVE MIDFIELD   SCHEMER   CREATIVE MIDFIELD
(Stiles)   (Charlton)   (Peters)

STRIKER   STRIKER   STRIKER
(Ball)   (Hunt)   (Hurst)

A lot of bunkum has been written since that Alf Ramsey killed off wingers. It was not Alf's fault but the coaches who blindly copied him.

Alf settled on the 4-3-3 system because it best suited the qualities of his players. It called for a balance of skill, fitness, strength, stamina and character. England were far from the most talented team in the tournament but they were the best organized and every player willingly shouldered responsibility and put the team effort before any selfish motives.

After the silken skills of the Brazilians in 1958 and 1962 it was something of a backward step for football when England won the World Cup with as much sweat as skill. Alf Ramsey had achieved what he set out to do by making England world champions but there is no question that had he been able to call on wingers of the calibre of Matthews and Finney or Hancocks and Mullen he would not have selected 4-3-3 as his system.

To defend the World Cup in 1970, Ramsey felt that he needed extra strength in midfield to combat altitude problems and introduced a 4-4-2 formation that once again spawned an army of imitators.

Actually a more accurate description of the England formation so successful in 1966 would be 4-3½-2½ because Ball was more often than not playing a withdrawn role in midfield, working as a fetcher and carrier. By the time of England's mission in Mexico Ball had dropped all pretence at being a striker and had been pulled back to a full-time midfield position.

This is how England lined-up for that fatal match against West Germany in Leon, won 3-2 by the Germans in extra-time after England had squandered a 2-0 lead:

GOALKEEPER
(Bonetti)

	RIGHT-	LEFT-	
RIGHT-BACK	CENTREBACK	CENTREBACK	LEFT-BACK
(Newton)	(Labone)	(Moore)	(Cooper)

CREATIVE	DEFENSIVE		CREATIVE
MIDFIELD	MIDFIELD	SCHEMER	MIDFIELD
(Ball)	(Mullery)	(Charlton)	(Peters)

STRIKER   STRIKER
(Lee)   (Hurst)

It is my belief that had England played just one winger in Mexico, Peter Thompson for instance, they might have retained the World Cup. Brazil took the trophy playing 4-3-3, with Jairzinho proving just how destructive a winger could be.

The next important tactical manoeuvre was introduced by the West Germans and the suddenly devastating Dutch. They became advocates of 'total' football, a system that had all the best points of *catenaccio* but without the anchor of a totally negative attitude.

A major breakaway from the *catenaccio* system was that the sweeper became much more mobile and was allowed complete freedom of expression. Franz Beckenbauer showed the masterly way the job could be performed with his attacking forays from a deep position when helping to steer West Germany to the European championship in 1972 and then the World Cup in 1974.

The success of total football depends on a team having efficient all-purpose players, defenders who can attack and attackers who can defend. It involves expert covering and intelligent support play and can be performed well only by players with a keen tactical awareness as in the Beckenbauer-inspired Bayern Munich team and the Cruyff-motivated Ajax side.

Ajax, then under the shrewd managership of the Rumanian Stefan Kovacs, revealed that total football was a step forward from the old, sterile *catenaccio* when they soundly beat neurotic, negative Inter-Milan in the 1972 European Cup with two goals from the master, Cruyff.

The refreshing difference about total football is that the defenders are encouraged to be adventurous and progressive. Put in simple terms, total football is all about being numerically stronger than the opposition whether when attacking or defending. Players must get into positions that are the most advantageous to their team at that given moment. Total football is the *thinking* man's game.

There are, of course, other formations such as the 3-4-3 that Ron Greenwood introduced when putting the emphasis on attack for England's World Cup qualifying match against Luxembourg in 1977.

Ron shaped his side with goals in mind because England needed to win by five or six to feel satisfied. This is how they lined up:

GOALKEEPER
(Clemence)

RIGHT-BACK   CENTRE-BACK   LEFT-BACK
(Cherry)   (Watson)   (Hughes)

RIGHT-   CENTRAL   CENTRAL   LEFT-
MIDFIELD   MIDFIELD   MIDFIELD   MIDFIELD
(McDermott)   (Wilkins)   (Callaghan)   (Kennedy)

STRIKER   STRIKER   STRIKER
(Francis)   (Mariner)   (Hill)

England struggled to a 2-0 win, failing to hit their goals target because they got bogged down in midfield where there were too many men trying to do the same job.

With hindsight, I am sure Ron Greenwood would have played a fourth striker — preferably a right winger — and one less man in midfield. But when planning his strategy 3-4-3 obviously seemed to him the right formation to suit the players he had in his squad.

Ron quickly realized that 3-3-4 was the system more likely to disrupt the defensive strategy of Luxembourg and sent on striker Trevor Whymark as a substitute for midfield man Terry McDermott in the second-half. *He showed that a coach or manager must always be ready to adapt a system when things are not going smoothly.* I am sure he wished he had a right winger on the substitute's bench whom he could have sent on to give extra width to the attack and stretch the Luxembourg defence so that it would have eased the traffic jam in the middle.

At the risk of sounding like a parrot, I want to emphasize once again the importance of choosing a formation that suits the quality of the players you have available and bear in mind the strength and likely tactics of your opponents. Ron Greenwood would not have risked playing a back line of just three defenders against a team capable of mounting sudden attacks. He knew that Luxembourg would use eight or nine men in defence and planned accordingly.

Any plan you have is only as good as the players operating it. Stress to each individual player that, without neglecting his major role, he should look for every opportunity to help the team performance.

The Sweeper

To play a sweeper in your defence the *catenaccio* way is like taking out an insurance policy. Played properly, it means you always have a spare man at the back as a reserve defender who 'mops up' in moments of crisis.

The back four defenders play a man-to-man marking system, each with a specific task of stifling the progress of an opponent. This creates one-against-one situations and the employment of a sweeper is a way of providing cover.

This system of course commits you to playing six defenders (counting the goalkeeper) and in Italy I have often seen two midfield men briefed to play defensively in front of the back line of four.

'Sweeping' is a specialized job that should only be trusted to a player with the right qualities. First and foremost he must be a quick reader of situations with a good tactical awareness. *He must be a master of interception, the incisive tackle and should know just when to push forward into the back line to take over as a marker if one of his team-mates has gone forward on an attack.*

It is not an easy strategy to employ and requires a lot of hard work in training matches so that the defenders get a complete understanding of each other's needs and responsibilities.

One of the best exponents of the sweeper role in my view was West Germany's Willi Schulz who was a key man in their 1966 World Cup team. He

Diagram 21 This shows the sweeper system. The sweeper (S) patrols the width of the pitch behind his back-four defenders who concentrate on man-to-man marking against the four forwards (A, B, C, D). If any forward breaks through, the sweeper moves swiftly to the danger area to plug the gap.

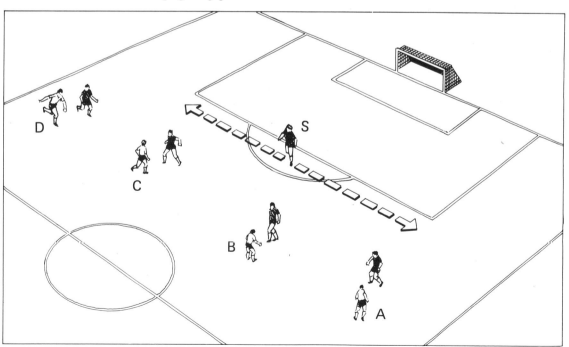

Franz Beckenbauer... always composed under pressure and seeking the chance to come forward from his 'sweeper' base as an extra man in attack.

patrolled the full width of the pitch to give strength in depth wherever it was needed most and always tried to be positive with his passes which turned defence into sudden attack.

For the sweeper system to be really effective, all the defenders — and in particular the full-backs — must accept the responsibility to take opportunities to move up into attack in a bid to get an extra man into opposition territory. The full-backs must be on the look out for the chance to make overlapping runs, confident that they will be covered by their sweeper.

Giacinto Facchetti was a master of full-back play with the Inter-Milan and Italian international teams that perfected the sweeper strategy. He knew just when to come speeding down the left wing into an attacking outside-left position and was often a more menacing front player than the strikers.

The difference between the sweeper role in 'total' football as opposed to *catenaccio* is as much an attitude of mind as anything.

Players such as Franz Beckenbauer and Holland's Arie Haan (very effective in his emergency role as sweeper in the 1974 World Cup Finals) think only how they can use their position at the back of the defence as a launching pad for an attack.

From the moment Beckenbauer was in possession, he would look to come forward. Sometimes he would carry the ball himself or exchange one-two passes with a midfield colleague.

What he was setting out to achieve each time was to move forward from his sweeper base and so in effect become an extra schemer for the attack.

Under pressure, he was an extra man at the back of the defence. Coming forward, he was an extra man in attack. It takes a special kind of player to be able to perform this role with full effectiveness.

Another way of operating a sweeper system is to have a defensive player moving across the front of the back line of four defenders. This was a strategy that worked well for England in the 1966 World Cup when Nobby Stiles patrolled the width of the midfield. His job was to intercept and win the ball with fierce tackles before the opposition could penetrate the heart of the defence where Jack Charlton and Bobby Moore had such a fine working relationship.

It is a method that has been much preferred in British football. The advantage is that the midfield anchorman can quickly position himself to join in the attacks. The disadvantage is that with no sweeper at the back an opposition player is through for a strike at goal once he has cleared the back four.

How YOU play depends on a) the strength of your squad; b) the strength of the opposition; c) the match result required.

Marking

There are two basic methods of trying to stop the opposition infiltrating your territory: man-to-man marking and zonal marking.

Man-to-man marking is easy to understand, easy to operate but can be suicidal. Each defender has the responsibility of marking one specific opposing forward, policing him throughout the game and making sure he does not have time or space to be creative.

But where it can go seriously wrong is if you are not playing the negative sweeper system and one or two of your defenders are up against opponents who are superior. The man-to man marking method can then become a disaster because a defender has no cover once he has been beaten.

The important rules for a defender to remember when on man-to-man marking duty is 1) never to commit himself to a tackle unless certain he is going to win the ball; 2) give a team-mate cover if it is possible without leaving his own opponent free to cause problems; 3) don't ball watch . . . always have an eye for the opponent because he can find space in a split-second.

Ball-watching is one of the most common 'crimes' of defenders, even at the highest level of football. Time and again you see a defender watching a ball coming into the penalty area and when he gets round to his job of blocking his opponent he finds he has got free into space where he can receive the ball without hindrance.

Man-to-man marking by the back four defenders puts a lot of responsibility

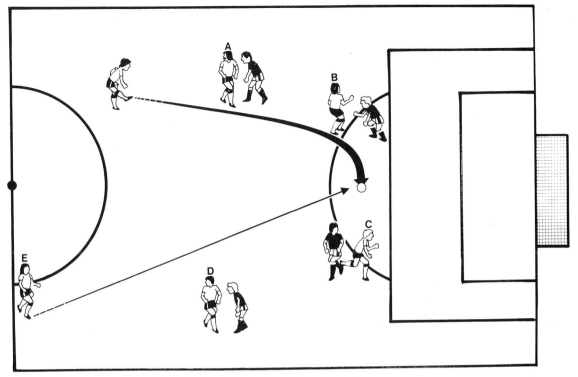

Diagram 22 This illustrates the dangers of man-to-man marking. Forwards B and C have drawn their defenders away from the middle and the ball is lofted over their heads to where E is making an unchallenged run. In a match situation, you would be looking for a midfield player to track back with E so that he is not allowed any space in which to manoeuvre.

on the midfield players who must come back when their team is under pressure and help out by covering and hassling the men in possession.

For this system to work correctly, the markers must be strong and confident in the tackle, disciplined and able to concentrate and act under severe pressure and be totally aware of what is happening around them.

Ideally from the point of view of being progressive, you should play man-to-man marking without a sweeper. But if you are in a position where you cannot risk defeat or feel that your markers are not reliable, then it is as well to have that spare man on duty at the back.

Zonal defence is an equally efficient and sometimes more effective method of protecting the goal. It calls for intelligence and thoughtful application and can only be operated by players who have full confidence and understanding of each other's play.

This system is about marking space rather than an opponent. Each defender has the responsibility of patrolling and protecting an area of the pitch. When that area is invaded by an opponent he must put him under pressure until he

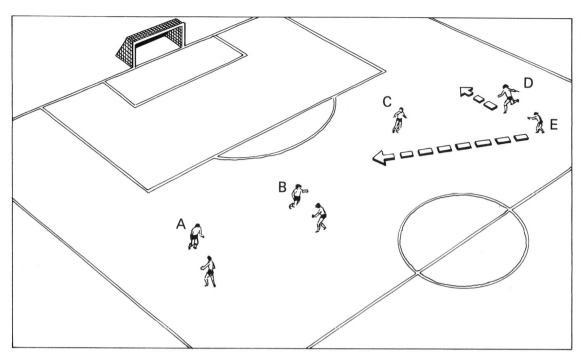

Diagram 23   Zonal marking. Defenders A, B, C and D have the
responsibility for patrolling and protecting a set area of the pitch. They
pick up any player who comes into their zone. If the opponent leaves his
area – for example, E moves into the centre – then defender D passes
him on to defender C.

has either won the ball or forced him into the zone of a colleague who must
then take over the job of marking the invader.

The success of the system depends on the speed of thought and action of the
defenders and their ability to communicate, to be on each other's wave length
when under pressure. This calls for an instinctive understanding which can
only be gained by constant practice with each other under improvized match
conditions in training.

What happens is that the defenders divide the pitch up among themselves
like a cake, each accepting the responsibility for an area where they will
challenge any attacking player irrespective of the number shirt he is wearing.

England operated the zonal defensive system superbly well during the 1966
World Cup. The dotted areas in the diagram on page 67 show where the four
back-line defenders mainly operated and the arrows show their directions of
movement.

To support this powerful back line, England had Nobby Stiles covering the
width of the pitch immediately in front of the back four. It worked so well
because all the players had intelligent tactical awareness and moved out of
their alloted zones only either to join in an attack or to cover for a team-mate in
emergency.

Like all systems, zonal defence has to be flexible. A defender must know the

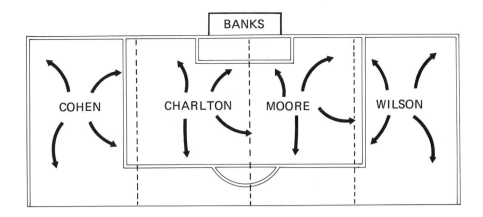

times when movement from his zone is necessary, such as to assist a team-mate who is confronted by a two-against-one situation.

It is important for the defenders to call to each other to help with the understanding and smooth operation of this system. When a player has allowed his opponent to move from one zone to another he must let his team-mate in that zone know whether he intends to stay with him. A simple call such as 'Take him' or 'Leave him to me' will do. All calls should be brief and clear enough to leave no doubts as to the calling player's intentions.

When practising this marking method, order your forwards to regularly inter-change positions with each other when making their runs in an effort to draw the defenders out of their zones. As soon as a defender intercepts or wins a ball he must be encouraged to distribute it with accuracy and imagina-tion. It will help if you have two or three linkmen patrolling just inside the halfway line to accept passes from defence.

Zonal marking allows a defender greater freedom to get involved in attacking movements. The man-to-man method is relatively restrictive on the defender whose position on the pitch is more often than not dictated by the movements of the player he has been briefed to mark.

Find out which defensive method suits your players best and then work hard at getting it right in training. The quality of your marking can mean the difference between victory and defeat.

The Midfield

The way I see it, the defence is the *backbone* of any team and the attack is the *head* and the *feet*. In midfield we have the *heart, eyes* and *brains*.

The midfield is where games are won and lost in modern soccer. It is the command post. Control it and you are on the way to victory. Concede it to the opposition and you will not be able to dictate the pace or the direction of the match.

I have discussed in Chapter One the ideal players for midfield. My intention now is to analyse how they are best deployed within the framework of your team formation.

To play the adventurous 4-2-4 you will need to have two very gifted midfield men. One would require all-round skills, the ability to tackle and win the ball as well as accurate passing technique. He would be the anchor man of the partnership, working between defence and attack wherever his services were most urgently required.

His partner would carry the responsibility of being the chief schemer and so would need to be a master at hitting long balls to any point up to distances of 40 and 45 yards. He must be inventive, imaginative and also know just when it will pay to release a quick, simple ball. Ideally, both partners should be proficient at shooting from long range so that they can take advantage of any openings for sudden sniper shots at goal.

It takes a bold team to play 4-2-4 these days because they are taking the risk of getting swamped in midfield by sides concentrating on 4-3-3 or 4-4-2 formations. If you are going to gamble on 4-2-4, it is imperative that the two flank runners up front should be alerted to coming back into midfield whenever the opposition is pushing forward.

A system I personally favour is 4-3-3, with two creative midfield men and an all-rounder who will have the dual role of helping out in defence and prompting the attack. The prime role for the two creative players is to provide a service and support for the three front runners, one of whom at least should be a forward who can make thrusting runs down either wing.

Throughout my managerial career, I have believed in getting width into my attack. I like to use at least one orthodox winger in the front three and an all-purposes player in midfield who can play the part of a withdrawn winger. His brief would be to patrol in midfield as a go-between for the front runners and to look for the opportunity to break down the flank with the objective of drawing the opposing full-back wide.

If you are playing against a team without specialist wingers, it will be the duty of your two full-backs to also get themselves into positions wide on the wings from where they can cross the ball into the paths of the central strikers.

When a full-back makes his overlapping run, any midfield player not involved in the movement should make a point of dropping temporarily into the vacant full-back position to prevent a quick counter attacking breakthrough in that unguarded area.

All midfield players should be made to appreciate that they have a defensive as well as attacking function and should practise the art of tackling and marking during training.

When you are planning your midfield strategy, remember that you need a balance of strength and skill. If you are playing 4-3-3 and all three of the midfield men are purely ball winners as opposed to ball users then you are going to find it difficult to create goals.

Circumstances will dictate your selection. You may be playing away from home where a tight-knit performance is needed and so will decide to tip the balance of the team towards defence, with two strong men in midfield flanking your creative schemer.

On the other hand you could be in urgent need of goals and so will play two creative men in midfield and one anchorman who will be encouraged to push forward at every opportunity.

If you are playing 4-4-2, I feel it necessary that two of the midfield players should be creative and accustomed to scoring goals. The more people who

Alan Ball... revealing here for Southampton the sort of midfield authority and control that first established him as one of the great dictators of the game with Everton and England. He is pictured going past Sammy McIlroy, himself a midfield maestro with Manchester United and Northern Ireland.

share the goal-scoring responsibilities the more options that will be open to your team when on the attack and the harder it will be for the opposition to lock them all out.

Creating a balance in your side is about simple mathematics. If you want to lean towards attack, then in a 4-3-3 system two of the three midfield players should be pushing forward and looking to make positive runs. That gives you five attacking players, with the third midfield player under orders to support in attack whenever possible.

By getting to know each other's play inside out in training, the midfield players can become a team within the team as happened when Alan Ball, Colin Harvey and Howard Kendall powered Everton to the League championship in 1970.

They were masters at supporting each other, making collective attacks from a midfield base and breaking down opposition defences with skilful inter-passing. By moving forward in group formation and pushing short, accurate diagonal passes to each other they always gave Everton depth in attack.

The Chelsea team that I steered to the FA Cup Final in 1967 had a well balanced midfield, with Charlie Cooke as the chief architect, John Hollins the powerful prompter of attacks and John Boyle as the anchorman. I always considered Hollins a model midfield player right from the age of 16 when I first put him in the League team. He was exceptionally fit, had plenty of enthusiasm and was always putting the team effort before any selfish motives. The only thing that prevented him establishing himself as a regular in the England team was his failure to score more goals. Perhaps if he had been just a little more selfish in his nature he may have become as effective as Billy Bremner was for Leeds and Scotland but he could never get out of the habit of passing when he was better placed for a finishing shot than the man he was feeding with the ball.

The great midfield players recognize when it is 'on' for them to score and with strikers so well policed in modern football it is becoming more and more important for the midfield men to find the back of the net.

To summarize, midfield players must look to be creative in attack, willing in defence and always ready to make supporting runs and to shoot for goal if they find they are better placed than the strikers.

The Target Men

Jimmy Greenhoff and Stuart Pearson had it at Manchester United when I was manager. Kevin Hector and John O'Hare had it at Derby County before I moved here. Peter Osgood used to have it when I introduced him to League football at Chelsea. 'It' is the gift for being able to make yourself always available to receive a pass in a crowded penalty area.

These sort of players are a midfield man's dream. Somebody he can always find with a pass and with the knowledge that when the ball is received it will be put to good use.

The modern term for the player who waits up front to receive the ball is 'target' man and his ability can decide whether or not your attack is going to function properly, with power and punch.

He is the central striker who often has to forage alone against a packed, unfriendly defence. Sometimes he has a plundering partner and by intelligent inter-changing of positions and hard and fast running they can drive a defence to distraction without the ball being anywhere near them.

The target man's main role of course is that of goal scorer. He must be a sharp shooter, powerful in the air and an opportunist ready to snatch at the

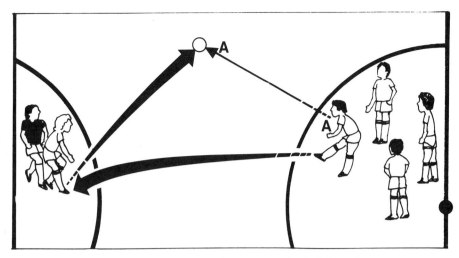

Diagram 24   Target practice. A player passes the ball from the
centre-circle to the target man who will be closely marked by a defender.
The target man's objective is to get a quick return pass to the player
who gave him the ball. Four or five players can take turns feeding the
ball to the target man, varying the speed and trajectory of their passes
and then running into space for the return ball.

half chance in crowded areas where movement is restricted and takes
courage.

Much of a team's attacking strategy is built around the target man or men.
As well as carrying the burden of having to score goals he must also make
them, holding the ball under the severest challenges until supporting players
arrive from deeper positions to receive his pass.

The perfect striker will always be looking to run into threatening positions
even when the odds are against him receiving the ball. Timing and positioning
are of the essence and it is vital to practise off-the-ball running in training, with
the midfield players pushing passes through as the strikers set off on runs into
a packed defence.

Much of what a striker does in the heat of battle is instinctive but his job
can be made easier with proper planning and preparation. Often what looks
like improvization has been carefully rehearsed in training.

Get your strikers 'selling' themselves in determined decoy runs to the far
post when the winger or overlapping full-back is in possession. The ball should
then be dropped short to the near post where a midfield player will have been
seeking to arrive at the same time as the ball.

*One of the most effective ways to disrupt a defence is with rapid, first-time
passing. A ball played quickly from defence to midfield and then transferred
immediately to the target man can set up a goal scorlng chance in seconds from what
had been a defensive situation.*

But this doesn't just happen in a match. It is an attacking strategy that has
to be polished and polished again in training, with a lot of sweat going into

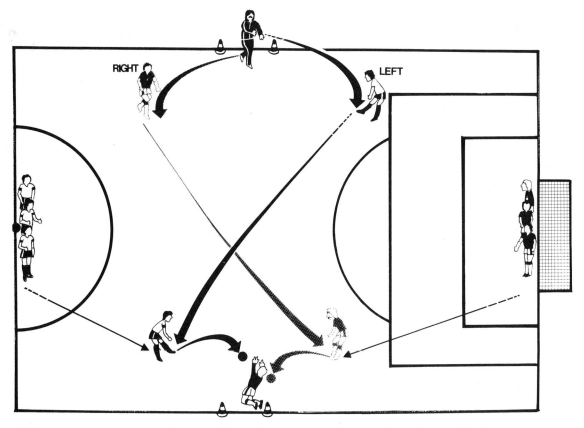

Diagram 25 A familiar training routine for professional footballers in preparation for the quick switch from defence to attack. The goalkeeper at the top throws the ball to the left-side midfield player. He fires the ball into the path of the target man approaching from the right who shoots at goal. The next ball is thrown to the right-side midfield player who passes to the target man on the left — and so on.

practice matches in which the emphasis is on one-touch football.

I close this chapter on soccer strategy with a description of a goal that shows what can be achieved by players schooled into knowing what to expect from their team-mates.

Scotland were playing Wales at Anfield in 1977 in a match that would decide which of them would go forward to represent Britain in the World Cup Finals in Argentina. The match was delicately balanced at 1-0 for Scotland when Kenny Dalglish clinched victory for the Scots with a gem of a goal.

It was the end product of a magnificent three-man move involving Lou Macari, Martin Buchan and Dalglish, all of whom had been regular members of my squad when I was in charge of the Scottish team. Macari and Dalglish had been a marvellous tandem team at Celtic and Macari and Buchan were later key members of the Manchester United team that I managed.

They knew exactly what to expect of each other as they advanced on the Welsh goal in the 87th minute of a memorable match. Macari was in possession in midfield and Buchan set off on an intelligent overlap down the right touchline.

Macari cleverly drew the Welsh defenders towards him before releasing a precise pass into Buchan's path. Dalglish knew what would be coming next and sprinted towards the near post past unsuspecting Welsh opponents.

The timing of his run was perfect — as perfect as the centre that arrowed towards the near post from Buchan's right foot. Dalglish smartly met the ball with his head to score the goal that took Scotland into the World Cup Finals.

It was a classic goal that summed up what strategy in Soccer is all about: GETTING PLAYERS INTO THE RIGHT PLACES AT THE RIGHT TIMES.

Don't turn your systems into straitjackets. Lay down guidelines for your players but don't suffocate them by restricting their freedom of thought and movement.

The art of successful Soccer strategy is to make plans that are flexible not fixed.

4
Tactics

Improvization and invention will always be the important hidden factor of football, something that blossoms at a moment's notice because of a player's particular skill or tactical awareness. As I have continually stressed in this book, I am all in favour of encouraging players to try the unexpected but the team that goes out on to the pitch with no set ideas at all is asking for trouble.

So we come to *tactics*.

I see tactics as getting players to act collectively to achieve a single end product. In attack, tactics are planned to create goals. In defence, they are about stopping goals; in midfield, they are about being constructive.

It would be suicidal for a team to try to play deadball situations by ear. For corners, free-kicks, throw-ins and general team play each player must be made aware of his individual responsibility and all the players must know the duties and movements of each other. It all has to be planned and polished in training. . . .

Defensive set-pieces

Defensive play is all about marking, covering, tackling and regaining possession with a view to launching a swift counter attack. Teams lacking good defensive organization when conceding free-kicks and corners are vulnerable to goals being plundered by a team that has worked in training on set-piece situations.

Let us first of all study set-piece positioning for CORNERS. The key defensive man is the goalkeeper. Because he has the advantage of being able to use his hands it is important that he places himself where he has the best chance of sighting and collecting the ball.

The goalkeeper usually prefers to station himself towards the far post and just off the goal-line. He must be given double cover, with a defender being positioned at each post.

It is the responsibility of the other defenders to mark tightly the opposing attackers. They must place themselves goalside of their opponents, far enough away to be able to watch the player and the ball but close enough to make the attacker feel cramped and restricted.

The goalkeeper should organize the defence because from his base he can quickly see the areas and players not properly marked. His objective will be to catch the ball as it comes into the goal area and he must shout to his team-mates to let

Diagram 26 Defensive positions for a corner-kick. The goalkeeper is just off his goal-line and stationed at the far post. Two defenders stand positioned at either post and three other defenders — A, B and C — stand goal-side and slightly forward of the men they are marking. From this position they can watch their opponents and the ball.

them know whether he is leaving the goal-line to gather the ball.

A goalkeeper's positioning will, of course, be dictated to some extent by the corner-taking methods of the opposition. If they are taking short corners or looking to drop the ball to the near post he may prefer to take up a more central base but still with the double cover of a defender on each post.

So that there is a minimum risk of misunderstanding a goalkeeper and his fellow defenders must continually practise corner-kick situations in training, with the attackers varying their corner-taking methods. The art of good defensive play at corner-kicks is to be properly positioned before the ball is kicked and to be prepared for swift adaption once it has been taken.

Defenders should mark man-to-man, with midfield players and forwards accepting that it is their duty to come back and pick up any spare men.

Even at the highest level you see teams caught napping in defence because players have not dropped back to help with the marking and covering at corners. A perfect example of suicidal slackness came in the 1977 European Cup Final when Borussia Moenchengladbach conceded a 'killer' second goal in the 65th minute against Liverpool.

Steve Heighway swung in a corner from the left and Tommy Smith sprinted forward to direct a superb header just inside the near post.

I would have awarded Tommy 10 out of 10 for positioning and alertness. But the Borussia defence would have got no marks for giving him a 'free' header at goal. Tommy's move upfield from his defensive base should have been spotted by a Borussia forward and when he arrived in the penalty area it should have been with uninvited company!

An important point to emphasize in training until it becomes instinctive in match situations is that defenders must move forward quickly once the ball has been cleared so that opponents are forced to retreat rather than get caught off-side. The goalkeeper should take the responsibility of shouting 'Everybody out' when he wants the goal area cleared.

Defenders have dual targets when facing corners: to mark an opponent and to win the ball. They must work in training at getting vital spring into their jumps so that they are able to get height for headed clearances. They must try to position themselves so that they can get a short run before take-off for their header. Few players can get sufficient lift from a stationary position and if they are standing still when the ball comes over from the corner they could be in danger of giving an opponent a free header at goal.

Opponents noted for their heading ability should be marked at corners by the defenders who are the strongest in the air. *If defenders find they are being outjumped, they must compensate by marking really tight and challenging as powerfully as possible.*

Opposing defenders coming into the penalty area for corners must be carefully policed by a forward who should alert a defender if he feels he cannot cope with him in the air.

I recall how Sunderland centre-half Charlie Hurley used to devastate Second Division defences in the 1962–63 season by trespassing into the opposition goal area at corners and using his height and great power to head spectacular goals. When I took Chelsea to Roker Park for a crucial promotion match near the end of the season we had a plan worked out to halt Hurley.

We put defender Frank Upton in a No. 9 shirt and briefed him to deny Hurley the time and space to set up attacks from the back. He and Derek Kevan were instructed to come back into our penalty area for corner-kicks to help our centre-half John Mortimore in the aerial battles with Hurley.

The result was that Sunderland's most menacing man was never allowed to make any impact on the match. Ironically, Chelsea won the game and clinched promotion with a goal from a corner that was scored by the smallest man on the pitch.

Little Tommy Harmer spotted Sunderland left-back Len Ashurst wandering from his position at the near post as Bobby Tambling took an inswinging corner-kick from the right. Harmer, with nobody bothering to pick him up, ghosted into the six-yard box and was unchallenged as he turned the ball into the roof of the Sunderland net with an unmentionable part of his anatomy.

It was a freak effort the way Harmer put the ball into the net but there was nothing lucky about the way he had got into the right position at the right time to take advantage of an elementary error of positioning by Ashurst.

When going through corner routines in training, make sure you practise clearances. It is pointless defenders just banging the ball away to any point in the field. They must be disciplined into *using* the ball with thought and intelligence. Any player not directly involved in defence at the moment of the corner-kick should position himself where he is easily available to receive the ball

A wall has eyes… Allan Clarke, Johnny Giles, Terry Yorath and
Billy Bremner show how alert you need to be when building a
defensive wall to face a free-kick in the goal area. An interesting mix
at club level: an Englishman, Irishman, Welshman and Scotsman.

ready to start a counter attack.

Defensive tactics at FREE-KICKS vary according to the position of the ball
when the kick is about to be taken. For a free-kick 35 or more yards out, the
concentration of the defenders should be on marking the attacking players,
forcing them to take up positions as far away from the goal as possible so that
the goalkeeper gets a clear view of what is happening.

From that distance the goalkeeper should be able to cope with a direct shot,
so the defenders must be alert to trying to stop the player who is taking the
free-kick from finding a team-mate with the ball.

If the kick is being taken out on one of the flanks, the defensive strategy
will be similar to that when facing a corner with all the attackers tightly
marked and the goalkeeper directing things from the back so that he can let
his team-mates know whether he is coming off his goal-line to collect the ball.
A two or three man wall can be built if the goalkeeper considers it necessary.
Should the player taking the free-kick find a team-mate with the ball, a
defender must quickly close down on the man in possession while the rest of
the defenders organize themselves to make sure nobody is free to receive a pass.

The closer the free-kick is to the goal the greater the threat of a direct shot
at goal. If it is within 30 yards and fairly central, a human wall must be
quickly built ten yards from where the kick is being taken.

The objective of building this barrier is to give the man taking the free-kick
as small a sight of goal as possible. The number of players in the wall depends

on the distance and the angle. There must be sufficient 'bodies' to guard against the shot being directed in the area of the near post. The goalkeeper will meantime be stationed where he can cover the far post.

As in all defensive situations, the goalkeeper is the man who must be in command of the positioning of the players in front of him. He must shout instructions to line up the wall to suit his vision and position.

It is vital that the goalkeeper has total concentration at the moment of impact so that he can immediately adjust his thinking and positioning if they attempt a different approach to a direct shot.

If the wall has been built properly, the player taking the free-kick should not be able to shoot into either of the top corners or chip the ball inside the far post. The goalkeeper must be alert to the possibility of a chip over the top of the wall to the near post and should be prepared for a swift movement across goal to cope with it.

I shall be taking a look at decoy methods employed at free-kicks by attacking sides later in this chapter and the only way these can be countered is by defenders being totally aware of what is happening around them. Safe defence is as much about thought as action.

It is essential that the wall is built quickly after the free-kick has been awarded. Try sticking to the same combination of players for the wall during training so that they get accustomed to lining up in a tight, well-organized barrier. The anchor man in the wall, the player who has the near post directly

Diagram 27 The wall. This is the correct positioning for a wall defence facing a free-kick being taken in a central position. The anchorman (A) is lined up so that the post is over his inside shoulder.

GOALKEEPER

A

behind him, must stand his ground no matter what.

He can be guided into position by shouted instructions from the goalkeeper who will let him know when he is exactly in line with the near post before taking up his position at the far post. A team-mate standing behind the ball can take a double check that the anchor man is positioned correctly.

The rest of the wall players line up inside the anchor man. They must ensure there is not a single gap in the wall and if an opponent gets in among them they should make it as difficult as possible for him to manoeuvre. The defenders must be particularly wary of him trying to move out of the wall at speed to leave a hole through which his team-mate can rifle a shot.

If the anchor man gets his positioning wrong, this throws the entire wall out and leaves the player taking the free-kick with the opportunity of trying to swerve a shot around the outside of the wall and inside the near post. It is a technique I shall be studying in the section on attacking set-pieces.

Any players not employed in the wall should make sure they are tightly marking the attacking players who are waiting to play their part in the free-kick movement should it not involve a direct shot at goal.

The defenders in the wall must be ready to move quickly forward in a tight group should the player taking the free-kick push a short pass to a team-mate. This will have the effect of not only distracting the man in possession but will also give him little time and space to place his shot.

Once the free-kick situation has been cleared it is important that all the defenders get back into their normal positions as quickly as possible. Improvize free-kick situations in training matches to get all the players well drilled in the respective parts that they must play.

As with the corner-kicks, it is imperative that players not involved in the defensive work should be positioned ready to receive the ball out of defence and so switch the emphasis of attack on to the opposition.

A well-organized side can create goals by using set-piece defensive situations as a launching pad for sudden counter attacks.

It is during set-piece manoeuvres that attacking sides are vulnerable to counter attacks. They have usually pushed extra men forward and so are stretched and understrength in defence. With quick thinking and decisive use of the ball, the defending side can exploit these situations the moment they gain possession.

Drum into your defenders the importance of clearing from defence with attack in mind. A long, positive pass accurately fired to an alert team-mate can set up a goal attack within seconds of being under pressure. The motto is a simple one to remember: Always try to turn defence into attack.

The objective of all defenders should be to make it as difficult as possible for the team in possession to use the ball to advantage. They must hustle and harry the player in possession while team-mates mark any players who could receive the ball.

Goals are generally only conceded because of defensive mistakes. Even the greatest goals can usually be traced to a defender either not marking properly, not covering, timing his tackle wrongly or giving the ball away in his own territory.

To defend properly takes great concentration, composure, discipline and enormous determination. And the *complete* defender will always be looking for the opportunity to trigger an attacking movement with a purposeful pass.

Urge your players during training to give as much study and practice to their distribution as to their defensive play. One of the main areas where British soccer has fallen behind the rest of the major footballing countries is in the use of the ball out of defence.

Tell your defenders to think of themselves as distributors. They must be encouraged to be constructive as well as destructive.

Attacking set-pieces

The hardest thing to do in football is to score goals. Great players of the calibre of Pele, Greaves, Law, Muller and Puskas could fashion them out of nothing. But many of the goals scored that look to be the work of a moment's inspiration have actually been carefully plotted and planned on the training pitch.

With defences becoming more and more dominant in modern soccer, the planning of goals from set-piece situations has become an important part of any training programme.

The more variations you have rehearsed for CORNER-KICKS the better your chances of being able to outwit the opposition. There are several alternative methods of taking corners and every member of the attacking force can be informed which one is about to be used in a match by a signal given by the player taking the kick.

Every team should have two or more specialist exponents of the long corner-kick. They must be adept at crossing the ball from a deadball position with outswingers that curl away from the goal or inswingers that can put suspect goalkeepers under severe pressure.

Your corner-kicking tactics will of course depend on the players you have available. It would be pointless sending long outswinging corners high across the penalty area if there are no tall men in the attack to take advantage of them.

If your players are being mastered in the air by the defending side they must look for different routes to goal. The corner taker can drive the ball hard, waist-high, into the goal area for a deflection or drop it short to the near post where a team-mate should be positioned for either a glancing header or a shot on the turn.

In training, it is vital to work on the positioning of the players in the penalty area. The bigger men are usually best deployed at the far post while the smaller, nippier players can be used for near-post running.

It is often an advantage to position a big man at the near post. He can block a goalkeeper's vision and can make a general nuisance of himself simply by taking up residence on the near side of the six-yard box.

England and Leeds used this tactic to great effect during the international reign of centre-half Jack Charlton whose powerful presence at every Leeds and England corner-kick became a familiar and even intimidating sight.

He scored a particularly memorable goal from a set-piece corner routine for England against Rumania at Wembley in 1969. What made it so noteworthy was that the man taking the corner from the right wing was his younger

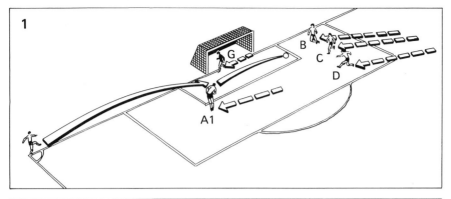

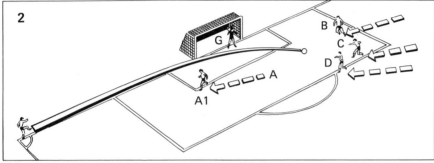

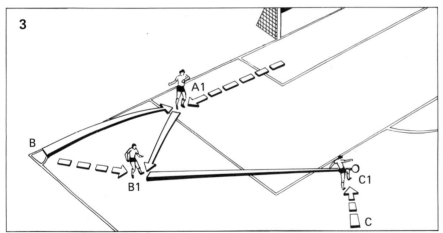

Diagram 28 Corner-kick variations: 1) 'A' has run from a central position to the near post and flicks the ball on towards the far post where 'B', 'C' and 'D' are all looking to get the ball into the net.
2) 'A' has again made a run from the central position but this time he is acting as a decoy. The ball is swinging towards the far post.
3) The short corner. 'A' runs from the near post to receive the ball and plays it back to 'B' who has moved infield to avoid being offside. To make a wider angle for the cross he plays the ball to 'C'.

brother, Bobby, who sent the ball curling in towards the near post where Jack outjumped the goalkeeper and two markers to steer a header high into the net.

Another variation is the short corner, the objective being to draw opponents away from the goal area and also for the corner taker and the man who has received the short pass to manoeuvre together to create a wider angle for a shot or a telling centre.

When central defenders move upfield to join in set-piece routines it is essential for other defenders to cover for them to guard against the quick breakaway attack by the opposition.

A *thinking* defender will sometimes delay his arrival in the penalty area for a corner-kick awarded to his team until the last moment. This could lead to an unwary defence not picking him up and an alert corner taker with an accurate kick could find him free, as happened when Tommy Smith headed that vital second goal for Liverpool from Steve Heighway's corner against Borussia Moenchengladbach in the 1977 European Cup Final.

The only way to perfect corner-kicks is with incessant practice, with the defence playing against the attack in improvized match situations. Work on all the variations until you find the ones that suit the strengths of your players best.

One of the most satisfying moments for a team is when a well-planned and imaginatively devised FREE-KICK produces a goal. The player who has scored gets the praise of the spectators but the team have the satisfaction of knowing it is the end product of a lot of creative thinking and hard labour in training.

It is particularly stimulating when you have managed to beat a wall defence, the human barrier that turns a free-kick into a challenge of power, skill and invention.

Such a goal that stands out in my memory came when the Chelsea team I was managing played West Ham at Stamford Bridge in 1966. West Ham built a four-man wall on the edge of the penalty area. Eddie McCreadie placed the ball for the kick and Bobby Tambling came running forward as if to take it.

The West Ham defenders braced themselves and then relaxed as McCreadie stopped Tambling's run-up and appeared to argue with him as to who should take the kick. They were still in deep consultation when Tambling suddenly pushed the ball through McCreadie's open legs into the path of John Hollins who fired the ball wide of the wall and into the roof of the net.

There had been some distracting gamesmanship involved but nothing outside the laws of the game. The free-kick procedure had been carefully worked out in training and West Ham had been punished for committing the cardinal sin of losing their concentration.

I remember us scoring an even cheekier goal in a Fairs Cup tie against Roma at Stamford Bridge the previous season. Chelsea had been awarded a free-kick just outside the penalty area and John Hollins placed the ball for the kick.

Terry Venables appealed to the referee that the Roma wall was not the stipulated ten yards away from the ball. He made a great fuss of pacing out the distance himself, holding up his fingers in mime of the count as he approached the Italian defenders.

The Roma wall parted in the middle as Venables marched purposefully through it. Then he shouted to Hollins: "Give it now, John!"

Denis Law... nobody knew what he was going to do next. He was an electrifying player in the penalty area and could fashion goals out of nothing.

Diagram 29 A simple free-kick manoeuvre. An attacker positions himself in front of the wall. The player taking the free-kick passes it to him and then quickly runs wide of the wall for the return ball and shoots first time.

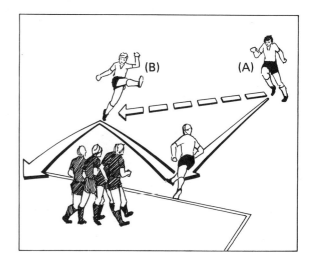

Hollins coolly stabbed the ball through the hole that had been opened and Venables fired it into the net for one of the three goals he collected that night.

Now I have not described these two goals to encourage gamesmanship and liberty-taking but merely to show the lengths to which players will go to outwit and out-think the defenders in the wall.

There are several ways to beat the wall at set-piece free-kicks. You can go around it, over it, through it or deliver the ball wide of the wall with a pass that will give a colleague an unobstructed shot at goal.

If your players have been trained and organized properly, they will have a distinct advantage over the defending side when they are preparing to take the free-kick. They will *know* what they are about to attempt while the defenders will not be able to react until the move is under way.

You are going to need players who will unselfishly act as decoys, knowing they will have only a walk-on part in the act of trying to score. The more distractions to disturb the defenders in a wall the better. There will be two or at the most three players involved in the actual job of trying to get the ball into the net while their colleagues make false movements and deliberately call for the ball knowing they are not going to get it. Everybody in the attacking area can help deceive the defenders into expecting everything but what actually happens. Successful free-kicks against wall defences are as much about the element of surprise as anything and they can only be performed properly after hours of hard but rewarding work on the training pitch.

Some of the greatest examples of how to execute the perfect free-kick came during the 1970 World Cup in Mexico when I felt privileged to be an on-the-spot observer of a procession of marvellous feats by the Brazilians.

I have an action replay picture in my mind of a superb goal scored against Czechoslovakia. The Czechs erected the usual defensive wall — six men in a tight line — to protect one side of the goal from a direct shot, while goalkeeper Viktor positioned himself on the other side.

Pele made a great show of collecting the ball for the free-kick and placing it on the spot, studying exactly where he was going to direct his shot. Then two other Brazilian players suddenly moved into the picture. Jairzinho distracted Viktor by placing himself as an extra man on the end of the Czech wall. He stayed long enough to get the Czech goalkeeper hopping about on his line in agitation and then suddenly moved towards the middle of the wall.

Meantime, Rivelino had been loitering behind the wall. As Jairzinho took up his new position, Rivelino — out of Viktor's sight — ran in a semi-circle towards the ball and struck it left footed with screaming power that sent it

Diagram 30 Rivelino's memorable free-kick goal against Czechoslovakia in the 1970 World Cup. This reconstruction shows how Jairzinho made space for the shot by moving away from the end of the wall.

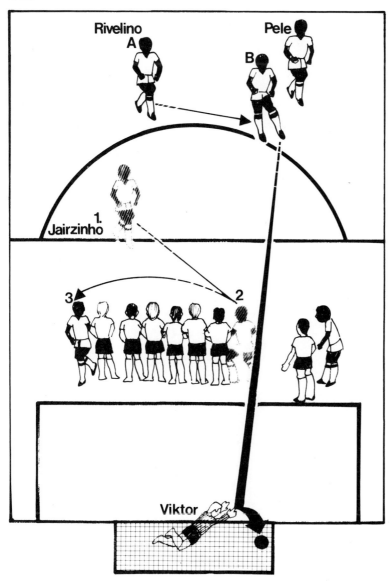

The wall survives…the fearsome left foot of Rivelino fails to breach the Scots defensive wall in the 1974 World Cup.

thumping into the net on a path to the left of the wall where Jairzinho had briefly placed himself.

Viktor, like nearly everybody else in the stadium, had been expecting Pele to take the kick and did remarkably well to get a hand to the ball as it flashed past him on its way into the net. It was Rivelino's goal but Pele and Jairzinho had played a part without touching the ball.

Four years later Rivelino and Jairzinho combined again to produce a spectacular free-kick goal, this time against East Germany in a World Cup group qualifying match in Hanover.

Jairzinho lined up inside the East German wall defence and as Rivelino raced up to the ball he ducked down almost into a sitting position. Rivelino's left foot shot was just high enough to clear Jairzinho's head and East German goalkeeper Croy saw the ball too late to stop it coming through the wall and into the net.

It was stunning in its simplicity but had obviously been well rehearsed and was the well-earned reward for ingenuity and skill.

There are only one in a million players with Rivelino's skill for bending, swerving and driving in shots that pack ferocious power. *But even ordinary players can pull off Brazilian-style tricks at free-kicks provided they have the confidence, the cheek and have been properly briefed in training.*

A free-kick that can be used to go over the wall is the 'mortar shell'. The player taking the kick chips the ball over the defenders into the unguarded space behind the wall. A team-mate will have positioned himself in the wall or at one of the ends and should be first to reach the ball simply because he has the advantage over the defenders of having advance knowledge of where it is going to drop.

Without apology, I recall yet another piece of Brazilian magic to reveal how a goal can be scored by going over the wall. This time my memory glows with a glimpse of the great Garrincha during the 1966 World Cup in England.

Brazil were playing Bulgaria at Goodison Park when Garrincha was chopped down about 25 yards from goal. Bulgaria lined up a wall of four defenders to guard the goal on the near side and their goalkeeper stationed himself at the far post.

It was conventional defensive play and there seemed no way the ball could be shot directly into the net provided the wall stayed firm. Garrincha and Pele seemed to be chatting about who should take the kick when Garrincha suddenly stepped forward and with his right foot sent the ball curving viciously over the head of the first man in the wall. By the time the ball had hit the back of the net it was in line with the last man in the wall. If the net had not stopped it, I reckon the ball might have done a tour of Goodison!

Not many players have the skill to get the ball up and swerving but two players working in harmony can achieve what a genius like Garrincha managed on his own.

I remember a well publicized goal against Manchester United just before I took over as manager at Old Trafford. Jeff Astle scored the goal for West Bromwich Albion but the main perpetrators were Asa Hartford and Len Cantello.

Cantello scooped a short free-kick into the air with the toe of his boot.

Hartford met it on the volley and sent the ball dipping over the heads of the defenders in the United wall. The ball smacked against the crossbar and Astle, knowing what his team-mates had planned, came following through to head in the rebound.

Try to bring a new dimension to the overall performance of your team by working to perfect a variety of free-kick set-pieces. Look for ways *through* the wall by parking attacking players among the defenders with orders to pull out a split second before the kick is taken so that a hole is 'manufactured'.

The players operating the free-kicks need to be quick thinkers and accurate users of the ball. If they decide to go *wide* of the wall as their route to goal they should cause as much confusion among the opposition as possible by stationing several players with known shooting ability in menacing positions.

If the player taking the kick intends to pass it square to a man on his left who is wide of the wall he must do his best to give the impression he is going to pass it to the player on his right.

The best exponents of these sort of free-kicks should hold an Equity card!

Give all your free-kick manoeuvres a code-name or a number so that what is about to happen can be quickly conveyed to the other members of the team.

While involving as many players as possible in decoy movements off the ball, it is wisest to keep the actual number of men who need to touch the ball as small as possible.

In training and in the matches, the idea is to try to get the ball from the free-kick spot into the net as quickly as possible before the opposition have had time to collect their thoughts.

So while all the off-the-ball movement makes it look complicated, the method of getting the ball into the net should be kept as simple as one man shooting or one man passing for a team-mate to shoot. Remember, the more passes that are made the more the chances of a breakdown.

Urge your players to be positive. Once they have decided on a plan they should stick to it, otherwise they could become even more confused than the opposition!

The throw-in

It has been estimated that throw-ins take up nearly one-sixth of the playing time in a match, so clearly it is a set-piece situation that needs as much concentration and care as must be given to corners and free-kicks.

I get irritated when I see teams literally throwing away their possession of the ball with careless, badly-organized throw-ins.

With proper preparation, every throw-in — even deep in your own half — can be used to launch an attacking movement. All it takes is accuracy from the thrower and intelligent movement from the receiver.

The tactics at throw-ins are similar to free-kicks in as much as the players must be prepared to act as decoys. Their positioning will dictate where the thrower places the ball. The receiver must make it as easy for the thrower as possible while his team-mates lead the opposition on false trails with their running off the ball.

Ideally, the thrower must try to get the ball to an unmarked player in space.

He can either return it to the feet of the thrower or make a progressive move towards goal.

The throw-in technique will of course depend on the area where it has been awarded. In your defensive territory, it is wisest to play safe. This can be done by a throw to the goalkeeper or to a defender standing deep who has time and space to make a decisive clearance. In a tight situation, the traditional 'line' ball is still effective. The ball is thrown as far as possible along the touchline, with the odds being that you will win another throw.

A point to stress to your players is that the man taking the throw can only be as progressive and as imaginative as the men who are waiting to receive it.

While it is nececsary to practise as many throw-in variations as possible in training, players should never lose sight of the fact that there are times when a quickly-taken, unrehearsed throw can catch the opposition off guard.

For the prepared throw-ins, you should have two or more specialist throwers who have been well schooled during training as to how to use the ball for any given situation.

Hold a pre-season throw-in competition to find which of your players are the best throwers, bearing in mind that you want accuracy as well as length. Once it has been decided who takes the throws, considerable time should be given to practising different methods.

If you have a long-throw specialist, a throw-in can become as useful to your team as a corner. When I was manager at Chelsea, I used to encourage John Hollins to perfect his long-throw technique. He could find the near post with a well-flighted ball and George Graham became adept at flicking it on with his head, sometimes scoring goals or creating a chance for a team-mate.

Then Ian Hutchinson joined Chelsea and took over the long-throw role from Hollins. Hutch was immensely powerful and could get the ball over to the far post with his windmill action. He used the technique to such devastating effect when Dave Sexton was manager at Chelsea that it won them the FA Cup in 1970.

Playing against Leeds United in the FA Cup Final replay at Old Trafford, Hutchinson hurled the ball from the touchline towards Peter Osgood at the near post.

Jack Charlton sensed the danger but was too hasty in trying to beat Osgood to the ball and succeeded only in back-heading it across his own goalmouth where David Webb bravely jumped to head the ball into the net at the far post.

The goal clinched victory for Chelsea and while the glory went to the head of David Webb it could not have been achieved without the hands of Ian Hutchinson.

The success of the long-throw depends on the length and accuracy of the throw and the positioning of the players in the penalty area. It would be a waste of energy and possession for the thrower to hurl the ball into the goal-mouth if his team-mates were not properly placed to make the most of it.

For every adaptation you work out for an *attacking* throw-in, remember to plan a *defensive* counter for it so that if the opposition try it against your team the players know how to stifle it.

The basic rule for defenders facing attackers at a throw-in is to mark tightly and beware of being drawn out of position by decoy runs. Players cannot be caught off-side direct from a throw-in, so defenders must be drilled into not letting attackers get behind them.

When I used to take throw-ins for Preston and Arsenal, I sometimes used the back of a colleague as a wall when I wanted to improvize a quick throw. There were even times when an unsuspecting opponent, with his back turned towards me, would suddenly feel the ball bounce off his back. Perhaps this might now be "Ungentlemanly conduct" but the lesson is that no player should ever turn his back on the man taking the throw.

Diagram 31   Throw-in variations. 1) 'A' and 'B' change positions in an attempt to get away from their markers. The thrower (C) releases the ball into the path of 'B' and will then race into space for the return pass. 2) The long throw to the near post after 'A' has made a decoy run towards the thrower. He then moves inside to receive a laid-back pass from 'B'.

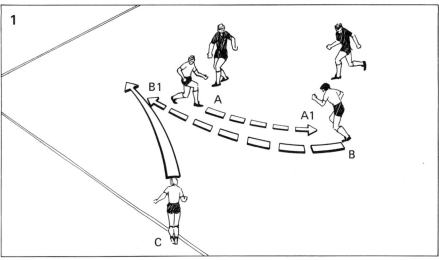

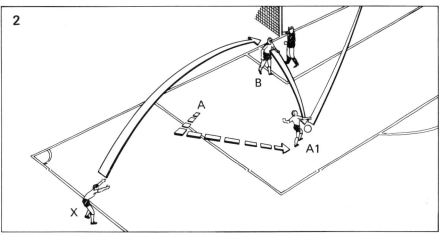

As with the free-kicks, good acting can help make a throw-in successful. A forward can make a decoy run towards the thrower apparently demanding the ball, while meantime a colleague runs into the position he has vacated to receive the throw.

Another simple tactic is for the thrower to release the ball to a team-mate and then move quickly into space to take a return pass.

The players waiting to receive the ball should all make themselves moving targets, inter-changing positions with team-mates to make it as difficult as possible for defenders to mark them and also to give the thrower as many options as possible.

With proper rehearsals, a well-organized team can make a throw-in nearly as useful a weapon in its armoury as a free-kick or corner. But like everything else, it calls for a lot of hard work in training.

The off-side trap

A well-drilled, alert defence can foil and frustrate attackers with smoothly operated offside tactics but it can be a dangerous game to play if one or more of the defenders is giving anything less than 100 per cent concentration.

The off-side Law states: 'A player is offside if he is nearer his opponents' goal-line than the ball at the moment the ball is played unless . . .
(a) he is in his own half of the field of play
(b) there are two of his opponents nearer to their goal-line than he is
(c) the ball last touched an opponent or was last played by him
(d) he receives the ball direct from a goal-kick, a corner-kick, a throw-in or when it is dropped by the referee.'

The first thing all players should be encouraged to do is study this Law until they fully understand it. Many spectators don't fully appreciate the full meaning of the Law and I have come across players even in professional football who are not completely sure of it.

To make the off-side trap work, defenders must work in unison. The objective is for the back line of defenders to move up together towards the halfway line to suddenly isolate an opponent just before one of his team-mates makes a forward pass.

The timing of the movement has to be exactly right or they are running the risk of giving their opponent a free run at goal. If they move up after the release of the forward pass, the opponent will be onside. They must also be alert to smart attackers making delayed runs from their own half to chase balls played into the space behind the line of defenders.

It is obviously easier to operate the trap if your team is playing with a spare defender at the back because there are situations where an opponent can be played off-side by just one player moving forward. The collective off-side trap is much more difficult to put into practice and it requires good understanding among all the defenders.

This can only be achieved by intensive training, with your midfield and attacking players trying to beat the offside trap in practice matches.

The most common method of catching opponents offside is for the defenders to race out from the goal area after the ball has been cleared. The danger here is that if an opponent has collected the clearance he could try to dribble his way through and put himself onside. He must be challenged by the nearest defender who should be careful not to commit himself to a tackle that could let the opponent through.

It is a good idea for the last defender who moves forward to shout 'Offside!' to attract the attention of the linesman and/or referee. *Offside traps played at speed often call for hairline decisions and it can help to alert a linesman whose attention could perhaps have been diverted at a crucial moment.*

But it doesn't pay to dispute the decisions of the referee or linesmen. It will help the overall team effort if players accept all decisions and play to the whistle. Goals are often conceded when defenders become 'frozen' in offside traps waiting for a flag that is never raised or a whistle that is never blown. If the trap fails to work, players should be ready for quick recovery work in defence.

Goalkeepers must be ready to back up defenders operating the off-side trap. They should be looking to come off their line quickly to deal with any through passes that may have bisected the back line.

The attacking team facing offside tactics must encourage players to make runs from deep positions. Midfield players and defenders can often come through on undetected runs to catch out defenders who have eyes only for the front attacking players.

Forwards who have good basic speed can beat the trap by running at an angle across the face of the back line of defenders, accelerating once the ball has been delivered into space and catching the defence square and on the turn.

The timing of their run has to be spot-on otherwise they will find a controlled defence has trapped them into an isolated, offside position.

Off-side tactics are a battle of wits, with *concentration* being the important factor.

Penalties

There is no set technique for the taking of penalties. Some players like to stroke the ball. Others blast it with full power. In many situations, a penalty is as much a test of nerve as skill.

I was responsible for conceding one of the rare penalties awarded in an FA Cup Final at Wembley. The referee, harshly in my view, awarded a spot-kick to West Bromwich Albion after Ray Barlow and I had collided in the Preston penalty area during the 1954 Final.

Ronnie Allen, an outstanding spot-kick specialist, looked the coolest man on the pitch as he placed the ball on the spot. Albion were trailing 2-1 and suddenly the enormity of the task he was facing must have seeped through to Allen because as he walked forward to take the penalty he stubbed his shot.

Our goalkeeper, George Thomson, dived to smother the ball and Ronnie Allen covered his eyes with his hands in his anguish. He was probably the only man in the Stadium who did not see the ball roll out of Thomson's grasp and trickle slowly over the goal-line! Albion went on to win the match and the Cup with a goal from the last kick of the match.

It just proved that with penalties anything can happen!

It is important to select the right player for penalty duty. He should have character and confidence and the ability to place a ball accurately even when gripped by tension.

The best penalty taker in training sessions is not necessarily the right man for the job under match pressure. It is relatively easy to slot the ball into the net when the outcome does not matter.

You can manufacture tension in training by introducing a competitive element. Hold penalty competitions, with points for the most successful spot-kick specialists. Give, say, three points if the ball goes into the net without the goalkeeper getting a touch . . . two points if the goalkeeper gets a touch . . . one point if it hits the woodwork before going into the net.

The best penalty takers manage to shut themselves off from the atmosphere around them. They refuse to be distracted by any gamesmanship from the opponents and have it clearly in their minds where they are going to place their shot.

Most of all, they must be positive. Any indecision will give an immediate advantage to the goalkeeper who will be doing all he can to gain a psychological hold in what is a cat-and-mouse duel.

A lot of bluffing and counter-bluffing goes on but the penalty taker holds most of the cards because he knows where he is going to place the ball. The goalkeeper can only guess.

Shots aimed low inside a post or high into one of the corners are the most effective and give the goalkeeper least chance of saving.

The rest of the team must not idle when they are waiting for a penalty to be taken. The forwards of the attacking side should be braced for a dash into the goal area in case the ball is pushed out by the goalkeeper. But they must be careful not to be caught off-side.

Defenders from the team who have been awarded the penalty must stay back just inside their own half ready to hold off any threatened counter attacks should the goalkeeper manage to get the ball quickly back into play.

And, of course, the defending side must be fully prepared to take advantage of the situation should their goalkeeper save the penalty.

Professional players should never miss from the penalty spot but it is surprising what can happen when the pressure is at a peak. Defending sides are always demoralized by the award of a penalty but they must convince themselves that all is not lost until the ball is in the net. With this sort of attitude they will be ready to launch a counter attack should the goalkeeper or the woodwork get in the way of the ball. Or should the tension get the better of the man taking the penalty.

5
Captains and Substitutes Home and Away Tactics

A good captain is much more than somebody who leads the team on to the pitch and tosses the coin. This is just the *easy* part of his job.

As a former captain of Arsenal and Scotland, I feel I know more than most about the right requirements for an effective skipper. Considerable thought should be given to selecting the right man for the job. A wrong decision can lead to dressing-room unrest and a loss of team spirit and confidence.

The first thing I look for in a captain is character. He must have the respect of his team-mates.

He should be captain in much more than just title. He will have full responsibility on the pitch for tactical changes and must therefore have a football brain.

I would expect my captain to inspire by example. He must never let his chin drop on to his chest no matter what is going on around him. I like to see a captain shouting at his team-mates but taking care not to make any of them look small.

Out on the pitch, the captain becomes the spokesman for the manager. He needs to have a strong personality and the ability to understand the character of individual players so that he knows whether to motivate them by blunt language or gentle persuasion.

The oldest player, the most experienced or the most talented is not necessarily the right choice.

Age doesn't enter into it. I made Terry Venables captain of Chelsea when he was 20 because at that time I thought his confidence and bubbling personality was what the team needed. It worked well for a couple of seasons but then I felt a change was necessary and replaced Venables with Ron Harris, who was a more steadying influence on the team. He was not as extrovert as Venables but he thrived on the responsibility and his attitude and total commitment to every game was an inspiration to his team-mates.

If two or more players in your team are equally well qualified as regards personality, character and knowledge of the game, the captaincy should preferably be given to a midfield player or one based at the back of the defence. A midfield player is ideally placed for leadership because he covers the go-between territory linking defence and attack and has an overall view of the match action.

In moments of dispute, it is the captain – and only the captain – who should approach the referee and put the team's point of view in a civilized and gentlemanly manner. Mass protests lead to a breakdown of team discipline and earn only reproval from firm referees.

The complete captain does not think his work is finished at the final whistle. He also tries to make himself useful off the pitch. Some clubs like to have a team captain and a club captain but the job of captaincy on and off the pitch is often combined.

He should act as the mouthpiece for his team-mates when any general discussion is necessary between club officials and the players.

I had an ideal manager-captain relationship with Billy Bremner when I was in charge of the Scottish international team. Billy was a driving, demanding skipper who did so much to make Leeds United a powerful force in football. He carried this same competitive spirit with him on to the pitch as Scotland's captain and lifted the players around him with his infectious enthusiasm.

Billy was an extension of me on the pitch. He knew the way my mind worked and what tactics I wanted employed. There was little I could do to influence the team once they had gone out on to the pitch but Billy and I worked so closely together on the pre-match planning that I knew I could rely on him to take command and make any changes necessitated by the events of the match.

The captain is the chief spokesman on the pitch but he must not be the only player who uses his voice. Calling is an important part of football and intelligent vocal communication between players can mean the difference between success and failure.

Confident calling between players helps team work and can have a great psychological effect, keeping a team on its toes and demoralizing the opposition.

It is often impossible for a player in possession to know what is going on around him. A shouted instruction from a colleague better placed to see what opportunities are available can help the player with the ball make the most of the situation.

Any calls should be clear, concise and positive. A referee can penalize a player for a shout that distracts an opponent so stress that any calls should be brief and clearly intended as an instruction to a team-mate.

If a crowd at a League game could be silenced, spectators would be surprised at the amount of shouting that goes on between players. The most common calls you will hear are brief warnings and instructions such as 'man on', 'keeper's ball', 'leave it', 'give it', 'mark him', 'cover me', 'hold it', 'first time' and 'that's mine'.

To avoid the danger of being accused by a referee of deliberately distracting an opponent, it is as well for the players to use a name when shouting. 'Leave it, Harry' would be an instruction that would not be open to any misinterpretation . . . provided Harry was the name of the player being advised to leave the ball!

Of course, there are times when players would be best advised not to shout. Ill-timed, unintelligent calling can alert opponents to a situation that they may not have seen. Players should only shout when it will help the progress of the team.

96

Make yourself heard...Jack Charlton never used to leave his
team-mates at Leeds in any doubt about what he thought. Calling is
an important part of football and intelligent vocal communication
between players can be vital to a team's performance.

Substitutes

Modern Soccer is a 12-a-side game, and even 13-a-side in some European competitions. Substitutes have become as important as any other members of the team.

The selection of the substitute should be calculated according to the circumstances of each given match. The venue, for instance, can decide the type of player you will have sitting on the touchline bench.

Playing away from home in a crucial game could mean that a defender as the nominated substitute would be more beneficial than an attacker. A team is more apt to be cautious away from home and so a defensive player would be best suited to the situation.

In a home match, it is usually wisest to have an attacking player as the substitute. It can give a psychological lift to a team to have a goal-minded player coming into a match at a critical time, as has been proved time and again by Liverpool's intelligent use of striker David Fairclough as a substitute.

The first job of a manager or coach should be to educate his players into accepting that the substitute system is for the good of the team. It was 1966 before substitutes were first introduced into British football and even now some players and many spectators have not learned to accept the system as part and parcel of the game.

I had to take some terrible stick from uninformed fans when in two successive FA Cup Finals with Manchester United I made the decision to send David McCreery on as substitute for winger Gordon Hill.

Each time it was a decision triggered by the tactical needs of the team. It was nothing personal against Hill. I considered his stamina at Wembley slightly suspect and felt that McCreery's freshness and pace would give the team extra driving power in the last 20 minutes of each Final.

There are many reasons for the substitute being used. The obvious one that the spectators understand is for injury but tactical changes often bewilder them and it is up to players to accept them as they are intended and without shows of petulance.

On occasions I have taken off a player who is having an effective match. Each time I have replaced him with a substitute who has gone on with specific orders to do a certain job, such as to pick up an opponent who is causing particular problems or to take on a defender whom we have noticed can be beaten in a certain way.

With the introduction of substitutes, managers can now take calculated risks with players who have passed late fitness tests. They can make sure they are covered in the event of a breakdown by having adequate cover on the sub's bench.

It is usual to select a team that is the strongest and best suited for the occasion. The substitute should be summoned into the match only if necessary and then with as few positional alterations as possible.

Make sure that the substitute feels part of the team. Include him in the team talks and make it clear to your players that he is there to be used if it is considered necessary. During the match he should sit next to the manager, coach or trainer and give 100 per cent concentration to what is happening on the pitch so that he can quickly click into the action if he is summoned to join the team.

The timing of sending on a substitute for tactical reasons is all important. Two of the worst-timed substitutions I have ever seen in major matches both involved Sir Alf Ramsey when he was England's team manager.

I have enormous respect for Sir Alf's tactical knowledge and his contribution to British football. But he struggled to get used to the substitute system simply because when it was introduced he was not involved in week-by-week matches with a club side.

Consequently, when he was faced with having to make substitutions in international matches he did not have the experience of knowing how best to implement the system. I felt his substitution of Bobby Charlton against West Germany in the 1970 World Cup quarter-final in Leon cost England the match.

Sir Alf's decision to replace Charlton with Colin Bell had already been taken when Franz Beckenbauer pulled Germany back into the game with a shot that deceived goalkeeper Peter Bonetti and went into the net beneath his diving body.

England, from leading 2-0, were suddenly struggling at 2-1 and the Germans had been given the enormous psychological lift of seeing their most feared opponent pulled off the pitch.

I understand that Sir Alf had wanted to save Charlton for the semi-finals but he had been having an exceptional game and his withdrawal pumped sudden hope and ambition into a German side that had looked beaten.

Sir Alf then sent the intimidating Norman Hunter on for the elegant Martin Peters but it was too late to stop West Germany's substitute, winger Jurgen Grabowski, from running the England defence silly.

Uwe Seeler snatched an equaliser and Gerd Muller scored an extra-time winner following a fast, tricky run from Grabowski. The turning point of the match could be traced back to Bobby Charlton's surprise withdrawal. It was a substitution that back-fired on England. Here was a lesson for all managers that to take off the wrong man at the wrong time can be suicidal.

Three years later, when England played Poland in a vital World Cup qualifying match at Wembley, I got the feeling that Sir Alf had still not fully grasped the substitute system.

After an hour of deadlock, it was obvious that England needed a left-sided player to open up the suspect area of Poland's deep defence. Sir Alf tried pushing Norman Hunter forward into an attacking role but he was clearly not creative enough to do the required job.

The score was stuck at 1-1 and England were on the way out of the World Cup when – with just two minutes left to play – Sir Alf at long last sent Kevin Hector on to attack down the left side. Even in that short space of time, Kevin nearly snatched a winning goal when he knocked the ball just inches the wrong side of the post.

The timing of the substitution bordered on the farcical. I can only imagine that in the tension of the moment Sir Alf lost track of time. Another lesson: always have somebody armed with a watch so that you can be informed how many minutes are left. As I say, the timing of your substitution is all important.

No player likes to be called off because the act of substitution is wrongly associated with failure. It is essential to make your players understand that any substitutions are made with the good of the team in mind.

It is sometimes a useful tactic to use your substitute as a psychological factor. Get him to go through a warming-up routine on the touchline This can act as a sudden warning to the players to produce maximum effort and enthusiasm.

When preparing to make a tactical substitution, the manager should first of all satisfy himself that the players he intends to leave on the pitch are all fit and able to play a full part until the final whistle.

Have a relay message system worked out so that any player who feels he needs to come off can let the manager or coach know on the touchline.

Remember that for a tactical substitution to have any real chance of being effective, it should be made at least 15 or 20 minutes before the final whistle. This will allow for the other players to adjust to the substitute's arrival and for any change of tactics to be properly implemented.

To protect the pride of a substituted player, encourage the on-going man to shake his hand as they cross. The manager or coach should then invite the player who has come off to sit on the touchline bench and so still feel part of the team and of the match.

Make sure that you have a blanket, sleeping bag or tracksuit to keep him warm. Try not to let him go off on his own to the dressing-room and brood.

Even the greatest players have to get used to being substituted. Ask Bobby Charlton!

Home and away tactics

Good organization and understanding in defence is essential for any team that seeks success at top level but I am firmly of the opinion that too many managers and coaches become neurotically preoccupied with not losing. This applies particularly to teams playing away from home.

The players go out on to the pitch so indoctrinated with defensive theories that when they are presented with opportunities to be positive they are shackled by pre-match orders that allow little freedom of expression.

I cannot stress strongly enough that your team should play to its strength whether it is at home or away. If it happens that your strength is based on defence, then that's the way to play it but encourage your players to use their defensive power as a springboard for launching decisive counter attacks.

But I see no reason in League competition for a side that has its strength in attack to adopt an unnatural defensive policy just because it is playing away from home. If you know you are going to be outgunned by the opposition, home or away, then you must work out tactics to curb their freedom to attack. But put as few restrictions on the natural game of your players as possible.

At Derby County, we like to consider ourselves an attacking side home and away. When we are on opposition territory I tell positive midfield players like Bruce Rioch and Don Masson to play their natural game. They are intelligent enough to know that if we are under pressure it is their duty to withdraw into defensive positions until we have regained possession.

Our simple theory is that when the opposition have the ball then everybody

100

but two front runners have to think defensively. When we are in possession, then everybody has to think positively. This is our policy home and away.

Fear of relegation forced me into thinking negatively in my first full season as manager at Manchester United. I went against my better judgment as the pressure on us mounted and ordered defence in depth. We went down at the end of the season.

We came back up as champions the following season by playing our free-flowing, natural attacking game. Looking back, I wish we had played to our attacking strength in our relegation season.

That's quite a confession for me to make and I say it only to emphasize that you should encourage your team to play naturally.

Stress to your forwards that often the best way for them to get involved in defensive play is in their opponents' half of the pitch. They should close down on defenders the moment they get possession and make it as difficult as possible for them to feed the ball through to the attack.

A cautious approach to an away match in a two-leg competition can often pay dividends, particularly in European tournaments when the opposition, the climate and the conditions may be unfamiliar.

If you have the first leg away from home, it could pay to have a supplementary defender on patrol in midfield as an anchor man. You can then be more positive in the home leg.

Your tactics in the away game if you have the first leg at home will of course be dictated by what happens on your territory. You may want to play defensively to protect a lead or with the emphasis on all-out attack in a bid to secure goals.

Home and away, I consider it best to concentrate on an attacking policy provided you have the players with the skill and ability to play positive football. But be careful not to give specific tasks to players who have not got the particular attributes to meet your demands.

I know many forwards who prefer playing away from home. They often find that they are given more room in which to manoeuvre because their opponents are pushing forward to support attacks.

In training at Derby, we concentrate in the week before an away game on exploiting these sort of situations. It is all about breaking quickly from defence. Don Masson and Bruce Rioch are both masters of making long and accurate passes.

They position themselves where they can be easily reached with a ball out of defence and practise finding the front runners with positive passes of 30 and 40 yards. The front runners must then make a goal attempt as quickly as possible.

To illustrate what can be achieved by a sudden break against opponents that are pushing forward in search of goals I go back to England's World Cup victory against West Germany at Wembley in 1966.

Bobby Moore and Geoff Hurst combined to score an historic goal that completed the first ever World Cup Final hat-trick and clinched England's memorable 4-2 triumph.

Germany had driven everybody up into England's half in a desperate effort to snatch an equaliser. Their furious attack floundered against the dominating

England defence and Moore was suddenly in possession deep in his own half.

Most players without Moore's quick football brain would at that late stage of the game have been looking to play it cautiously to ensure the Germans could not regain possession.

But Moore was a master at turning defence to attack and he had a strong and willing partner in Hurst.

Germany were completely committed to attack and they watched almost in slow motion horror as Moore struck a lethal 30 yard pass out of defence and into the path of Hurst who was motoring towards the halfway line. Willi Schulz and Wolfgang Overath were both goal-side of Hurst as he raced to receive the ball but were caught on the turn by the speed of the break.

Hurst controlled the ball on his chest and then set off on a run with Overath in desperate pursuit. Goalkeeper Hans Tilkowski dithered about whether to come out to meet the oncoming Hurst and by the time he had made up his mind found himself beaten by a rocketing left foot shot.

It was a classic example of what can be achieved with a sudden break from defence. Practised in training, it is a movement that can create goals out of nothing. Home and away.

Bobby Moore...showing the single-minded concentration that he gave to every game. His strengths were his reading of situations that enabled him to be a thought and a move ahead of opponents and his ability to switch defence to attack with a precisely-placed upfield pass.

6

Outstanding Club Sides

I have selected ten outstanding British club sides of the last 20 years to help me further illustrate some of the points I have been making in previous chapters.

They are not necessarily the top ten teams of that time but each of them had qualities that, put together, would produce the perfect team . . .

Tottenham 1960–61

They were understandably labelled Super Spurs when they became the first team this century to win the League and FA Cup double. I was more conscious than most of their stunning skills because when they were at the peak of their power I was winding down my playing career just two miles away at Arsenal.

We were haunted by them at Highbury where it was painful having to live in the shadows of such a talented team.

Bill Nicholson was their shrewd and knowledgable manager and he got the balance of the team just right. *They were well organized but individual players were allowed to do things their own way. Nobody was ever suffocated in that Spurs side.* Their line-up was a loose 3-3-4:

BROWN

BAKER   NORMAN   HENRY

BLANCHFLOWER   WHITE   MACKAY

JONES   SMITH   ALLEN   DYSON

The real strength of the side was in that middle line: Blanchflower-White-Mackay. Danny Blanchflower was the brains of the team, John White the eyes and Mackay the brawn.

All three were creative attacking players, Danny hiding his lack of real speed with intelligent positional play. White was a devil for defences to mark. He was nicknamed the Ghost of White Hart Lane and was a master at finding space. I was Mackay's wing-half partner in three Scottish international

The victorious Spurs double winning side parade the trophy after beating Leicester City in the 1961 FA Cup Final.

matches and can vouch for the fact that he tackled like a clap of thunder but also had a lot of skill to go with his strength.

British teams had not got hooked on the drug of defensive football when they were operating and Tottenham used to throw seven players forward into attack, with Blanchflower and White providing a procession of telling passes.

Their positive approach to every match is mirrored in their League record for that double season. They conceded 55 goals while setting a new post-war scoring record of 115 goals.

Bulldozing Bobby Smith and Les Allen were the main strikers, feeding off the unpredictable but effective runs of Cliff Jones and the industry of Terry Dyson.

Jones and Dyson (or Terry Medwin if either were injured) were fast-moving wingers who gave the Tottenham attack width. They used to specialize in

Jimmy Greaves…always a dangerman when the ball was at his feet. He had the peak moments of his career at Tottenham when he was in harness with first Bobby Smith and then Alan Gilzean.

106

drawing and turning full-backs before centring the ball where Smith and Allen were waiting to pounce. Smith disrupted defences with his enormous strength but had more skill than he was given credit for and was clever at receiving the ball and then giving a subtle little touch off to a team-mate before sprinting into position for the return pass.

Smith's skill was more evident the following season when Jimmy Greaves arrived from AC Milan as his playing partner. They quickly struck up a telepathic understanding and always knew the positions to get into to help each other.

Blanchflower, White, Mackay, Jones and Smith were the world-class stars in that Tottenham double team. But it was the unselfish work of the supporting players that helped shape the team into a championship combination.

Goalkeeper Bill Brown, an old Scottish international team-mate of mine, was an agile if sometimes unpredictable last line of defence. He had a good understanding with tall, commanding centre-half Maurice Norman who tended to be slow on the turn but had the strength of an ox and was dominating in the air.

Peter Baker and Ron Henry were not exactly world beaters at full-back but both played a prominent part in the team's success simply by giving every match their total effort and concentration.

Tottenham were among the last of the 'old school' of soccer and I include them in this book on modern tactics because much of what they set out to do on a football pitch would be stunningly effective in today's game.

They played with flair and imagination and were never afraid to attack the opposition. Their use of wingers to give the attack width and variety would be a practical way of getting around the back of modern defences.

How would that Tottenham team have fared in today's football? I think they would have been forced to play with more caution but they had so many gifted individual players that with a few adjustments at the back I feel they would have more than held their own. If they were in action in the modern game, Dave Mackay would doubtless have been pulled back alongside Maurice Norman — a role he performed with style and success when he dropped his buccaneering midfield role to patrol with Roy McFarland at the heart of the Derby County defence.

And to avoid being outnumbered in midfield, I reckon Bill Nicholson would have pulled that willing worker Terry Dyson back to make it an attack-minded 4-3-3 formation.

I don't hold with living in the past but I do believe we can learn from history. The lesson from that great Tottenham team is that outstanding individual players can be allowed total freedom of expression inside the framework of a well organized team.

They scored 115 goals while winning the League championship. Liverpool scored 62 when winning the title in 1976–77. There's a message there somewhere!

Ipswich Town 1961–62

I include Sir Alf Ramsey's Ipswich team not because I consider they were a great side but as an example of what can be achieved by good organization and playing to the strengths of the squad of players that are available.

Ipswich did not have a single player who could be rated as world-class. In fact when they kicked off in their championship season not one of the team had gained international honours, although centre-forward Ray Crawford was later to get his England chance.

On paper, Ipswich looked quite ordinary. On the pitch they were quite extraordinary! Alf built his team to a modified 4-2-4 system, nearly identical to the 4-3-3 formation with which he was to capture the 1966 World Cup for England:

BAILEY

CARBERRY   NELSON   ELSWORTHY   COMPTON

BAXTER   MORAN

LEADBETTER

STEPHENSON   CRAWFORD   PHILLIPS

Jimmy Leadbetter was the key man whose positioning baffled and bewildered many defenders not accustomed to playing against a withdrawn winger. Alf had him wearing a No. 11 shirt but patrolling in midfield from where he picked up balls from defence and splayed out passes to powerful twin strikers Crawford and Ted Phillips.

Roy Stephenson was a fast, orthodox right winger who stayed out on the touchline to pull defences wide and give Crawford and Phillips more scope and space.

This pattern of play worked so well that Crawford helped himself to 33 goals and Phillips collected 28 as Ipswich emerged as shock League champions.

The defence was under the command of Andy Nelson, a solid and reliable centre-half of the old school. Bill Baxter was a powerful anchorman in midfield, while Doug Moran quietly and effectively fed the attack with well-placed passes from his position as the central midfield schemer.

It was obvious while watching this team of 'nobodies' become champions that Alf had done his homework on the training pitch. *The Ipswich triumph was all about team work, with everybody willing to help and support each other. They were well conditioned both mentally and physically and were a wonderful advert for what can be achieved with the right combination of thought and deed.*

They proved that a team does not necessarily need outstanding individual players to capture championships. Provided the right creative thinking and hard work goes into the preparation for a game a team can grow in stature and confidence on match day.

The secret of the Ipswich success was preparation, team work and total belief in their own ability. I have often considered Sir Alf Ramsey too cautious and defensive minded in his approach to football but he motivated that Ipswich side into being positive and purposeful.

West Ham United 1963–65

This West Ham team of the mid-1960s was too brittle at the back to be classed as a great side but I have included them in this analysis because their attacking attitude was something I applauded and appreciated.

Their most formidable formation was a fluent 4-2-4:

STANDEN

BOND (or KIRKUP)   BROWN   MOORE   BURKETT

BOYCE   PETERS

BRABOOK   BYRNE   HURST   SISSONS

Eddie Bovington was a powerful anchorman in midfield in the 1964 FA Cup Final win against Preston before Martin Peters established himself in the team and Alan Sealey and Brian Dear were in action a year later in place of Brabook and the injured Byrne when West Ham won the European Cup Winners' Cup with an impressive victory over Munich 1860 in a memorable Final.

The three main motivators of the team were Bobby Moore, Geoff Hurst and Martin Peters, whose understanding of each other's play was an important factor in England's 1966 World Cup success.

But if I personally had to pick the star man of the side I would plump for the unheralded Ronnie Boyce, whose late headed goal against my old club Preston clinched a 3-2 victory in the 1964 FA Cup Final.

Boyce operated in midfield, working as an interceptor of attacks. He was not a particularly hard tackler but had a knack of winning possession by clever positioning and 'reading' what the opposition were about to attempt. Once he had got the ball he used it precisely and always with progress in mind.

Moore, Hurst, Peters and the creative Johnny Byrne were all international-class players but for me it was Boyce – always quietly busy – who gave the team drive and direction.

I rated Moore a great player for England but he was often made to look quite ordinary in a West Ham defence that used to come apart under pressure.

Peters was a luxury player, marvellous to have on your side when you were on top but tending to get lost when the opposition were in command.

But for all their deficiencies, this West Ham team was always attractive and entertaining to watch and I admired manager Ron Greenwood for sticking to his principles and insisting on positive play at all times.

They had some superb passing movements worked out and were really potent as a going-forward side. *Their use of the near-post ball was particularly devastating and is a tactic that all teams should have in their armoury.*

West Ham were a powerful left-sided team when they had John Sissons operating as an orthodox left winger. Moore, Peters, Hurst and Sissons all favoured the left side of the field and were difficult to contain when coming forward together.

Moore would fire the ball out of defence to Sissons who had the speed and skill to race on the outside of his full-back. Byrne and Hurst would set off on decoy runs to the far post, taking two defenders with them. Then Sissons would drop his centre short to the near post where Peters would arrive on cue for a goal attempt.

In their next raid, Peters would join Byrne in the decoy run to the far post and it would be Hurst presenting himself at the near post for the pass from Sissons.

The defence would just think they had got it worked out when in the next raid both Hurst and Peters would run to the near post and as the opposition defenders went with them Sissons would direct the ball to Byrne at the far post!

It was imaginative and intelligent football. And it had all been perfected in training.

Celtic 1966–67

The Scotsman in me cannot possibly let this chapter go without mention of the excellent Celtic combination shaped by Jock Stein.

The team that Jock built — with lots of ball training and with a heavy emphasis on attack — shone during an era when many clubs were turning to deep defence.

Quite deservedly, they became the first British team to win the European Cup and exposed the defensive disease that had eaten into Italian football while they were about it.

Early in the 1970s a new style and concept of Soccer was reported to have been developed on the Continent. It was labelled 'Total' football, a title that was supposed to reflect an attacking style that involved all the outfield players. Celtic had been among the innovators of this pattern of play in the mid-1960s but were not given the credit they deserved.

The success of that Celtic team was based on support running. Each time a Celtic player was in possession he had a man running intelligently off the ball making himself available to receive a pass.

Full-backs Jim Craig and Tommy Gemmell overlapped as a matter of course, the midfield men were always looking for opportunities to race forward into menacing attacking positions and the wingers were often seen back in their own half harrassing their opposite numbers.

They played a 4-2-4 formation but were never rigid or stereotyped. Attackers happily defended when it was necessary and defenders were continually hunting with the forwards whenever extra men were needed up front.

This was how Celtic lined up for the 1967 European Cup Final when they convincingly crushed the defence-dominated Inter-Milan team coached by Helenio Herrera:

SIMPSON

CRAIG   McNEILL   CLARK   GEMMELL

MURDOCH   AULD

JOHNSTONE   WALLACE   CHALMERS   LENNOX

110

Craig, McNeill, Clark and Gemmell made up a formidable back line in front of Ronnie Simpson, who was alert and agile for all his 36 years. John Clark played as a progressive sweeper, covering for big Billy McNeill and using the ball intelligently out of defence.

Bobby Murdoch and Bertie Auld were a well balanced tandem team in midfield, Murdoch playing with controlled power and Auld distributing the ball with precision and imagination.

Wee Jimmy Johnstone, one of the greatest wingers there has ever been when in the right frame of mind, could run defences into dizzy disarray before cutting back dangerous passes to the tireless Willie Wallace or pushing crosses into the path of the sharp-shooting Steve Chalmers. Out on the left, Bobby Lennox was a darting, thrusting player who was content to put the team effort first before any selfish motives.

Mazzola had given Inter-Milan an eight minute lead from a generously awarded penalty. It would have cracked and demoralized many teams but it triggered Celtic into revealing that they had character as well as style.

Inter-Milan, from habit, became ultra defensive after their early goal and Celtic unleased a barrage of attacks, with Gemmell making the most of his total freedom on the left to produce a procession of overlapping runs.

Gemmell finally got the reward his industry deserved when he fired in a spectacular equaliser from 20 yards. And it was Gemmell who again trespassed deep into Inter-Milan territory before making the pass for Murdoch to hammer in a shot that was deflected into the net by Chalmers.

Celtic won the match far more convincingly than the 2-1 scoreline suggests. They ran the Italians off their feet and their victory was a triumph for adventurous, attacking football over the negative, spoiling system operated by Inter.

Tommy Gemmell's performance provided a lesson for all full-backs who are facing a team playing without recognized wingers. *With nobody to mark, Gemmell concentrated on becoming an auxiliary attacker, moving down the left touchline at every opportunity to give Celtic width and an extra man in their firing line.*

This Celtic team was without question one of the greatest of all post-war British club sides. The balance and blend of the team was just right and they were able to cement an all-round understanding and confidence during their Scottish League matches where the pressure is never so great as in the English First Division.

In Jock Stein's first six full seasons as manager at Parkhead, Celtic won six League titles, reached 11 Scottish FA Cup and League Cup Finals and were twice European Cup finalists — beating Inter-Milan 2-1 in 1967 and losing 2-1 to Feyenoord in 1970.

It's a record that speaks for itself about the quality of the team that Jock built.

Manchester United 1967–68

Manchester United won the European Cup in 1968 with a team that was just past its peak as a great side but still with sufficient flair and fight to master an unpredictable Benfica side in an emotional Final at Wembley.

I include this United team in my analysis because they played with an adventurous spirit that sometimes bordered on the reckless. *And for the purposes of tactical lessons, Nobby Stiles gave a daunting demonstration in the Final against Benfica of how tight marking can suppress the most skilful of opponents.*

Stiles was briefed to give Eusebio as little space as possible in which to manoeuvre, a job he did with ruthless efficiency. There were some complaints that he was perhaps too rugged with his challenges but it was nothing to the rough treatment Humberto and Cruz dished out to George Best in the other half of the pitch.

I personally didn't like the Stiles style of defensive play. It was too much about being destructive and not enough about being constructive for my taste.

But at this level of football where winning is all important you just cannot afford to let a player of Eusebio's class have the freedom of the pitch otherwise he will destroy your defence.

Stiles patrolled just in front of the back line of defenders in this 3-1-3-3 formation at Wembley:

STEPNEY

BRENNAN   FOULKES   DUNNE
STILES
CRERAND   CHARLTON   SADLER

BEST   KIDD   ASTON

Pat Crerand and Bobby Charlton controlled the midfield with intelligent positioning and passing and Bobby was always seeking the chance to unleash one of his sudden sniper shots. David Sadler had two roles, filling in alongside Bill Foulkes when United were under pressure and pushing forward as an extra attacker when United were in possession.

With Best taking a battering every time he tried to weave through the Benfica defence, it was left to John Aston to emerge as United's most progressive and productive forward with jinking, darting runs that presented constant problems to the Portuguese defenders.

Brian Kidd, who celebrated his 19th birthday with a well-taken goal, played with plenty of enthusiasm and energy but I wonder if the game would have gone into extra-time if that superb opportunist Denis Law had not been injured.

A typically arrogant goal from George Best gave United the lift they needed in extra-time and they finally ran out comfortable 4-1 winners of a game that was too full of nerves and tension to be classed as a classic.

This was by no means the best of all United teams but their European Cup triumph was a wonderful boost for English club football and well deserved after all their years of near misses in this most demanding of competitions.

Bobby Charlton...controlled the midfield for Manchester United and England with intelligent positioning and pin-pointed passing and was continually looking for the chance to unleash a long-range sniper shot.

George Best...now helping to sell Soccer in the United States with the Los Angeles Aztecs. It was Best's typically arrogant goal that gave Manchester United the lift they needed in extra-time of their triumphant 1968 European Cup Final against Benfica.

Leeds United 1968–69

The League championship winning Leeds team of 1968–69 features in this chapter because of their outstanding defensive qualities.

They conceded only nine goals at home and 17 away during a season when they were beaten just twice in 42 League matches.

It is significant that Gary Sprake, Paul Reaney, Billy Bremner, Jack Charlton and Norman Hunter were all young members of the Leeds side that conceded only 34 goals when winning the Second Division title in 1964. They were still together five years later and their understanding of each other's play meant they were masters of covering and smothering goal attempts by the opposition.

Terry Cooper, a fine attacking full-back, replaced Willie Bell on the left side of the defence as partner to Paul Reaney and the versatile Paul Madeley was a regular member of the championship squad as a cover for almost any position.

With such an experienced squad of players, manager Don Revie was able to select his team and decide his tactics according to the strengths or weaknesses of the opposition. A typical Leeds line-up of that season was

SPRAKE

REANEY   CHARLTON   HUNTER   COOPER

BREMNER   GILES

GRAY

LORIMER   JONES   O'GRADY

Often when playing safe away from home, Revie would draft Madeley into a defensive midfield role with Lorimer or Gray standing down.

Reaney, Charlton, Hunter and Cooper were the backbone of the team, while Bremner and Giles were the heart. They ran away with the championship, beating runners-up Liverpool by six points.

They didn't win too many friends in football with methods that were sometimes over-tough but I admired their professionalism and the thoroughness with which they prepared for every game.

Giles gave the team vision with his intelligent positional play and long passes that were inch perfect, while the fiercely competitive Bremner was equally effective in defence and attack with his industry and total involvement.

The lesson to be learned from this ruthlessly efficient Leeds team is that the preparation for matches is as important as the actual playing of the game.

Every player knew the job he had to do and set about it with complete concentration and 100 per cent effort. The team was not adventurous enough for my personal liking but the impressive manner in which they carried off the championship proved that their methods were effective.

Everton 1969–70

Everton succeeded Leeds as League champions with football that was played with much more freedom and flair. They were so dominant that they left Leeds nine points behind in second place.

Their style was reminiscent of the *'push-and-run'* football with which Tottenham captured the Second and First Division championships in successive seasons back in the early 1950s.

The *push-and-run* system was devised by the then Tottenham manager Arthur Rowe. If anything, it was a fore-runner of 'Total' football and involved players giving quick, simple passes and then running into space to receive the ball.

I admired Everton's attacking approach to the game at a time when many teams had gone over towards the style of drab defensive football that had helped make England World champions in 1966.

Everton played to a 4-3-3 formation and often switched it to 3-3-4 by pushing Tommy Wright up on overlapping runs down the right wing:

WEST

WRIGHT   LABONE   HURST   BROWN

KENDALL   BALL   HARVEY

HUSBAND   ROYLE   MORRISSEY

Keith Newton was bought from Blackburn to replace Sandy Brown at left-back and to give the defence extra skill and strength for the run-in to the championship.

The main motormen of the team were the midfield trio of Kendall, Ball and Harvey. *They were a team within the team and would often come forward together in triangular movements, beating defences with swift inter-passing and sudden sprints into space.*

Kendall was the defensive anchorman of the trio but all three of them were adept at winning the ball. Ball played furthest forward, but they could all attack. Harvey was a master of positioning and nearly in Ball's class as a creative player.

Big Joe Royle was the chief marksman and impressively helped himself to 23 goals, feeding hungrily on the service of Kendall, Ball and Harvey and the clever left wing work of Johnny Morrissey. Jimmy Husband was a fast and eager support striker, with Alan Whittle giving useful service as a reserve member of the first-team squad.

They did not have the all-round skill of the championship-winning Everton side of 1963 that featured outstanding individuals like Alex Young, Tony Kay, Billy Bingham, Jimmy Gabriel, Dennis Stevens and Roy Vernon but their team understanding and overall organization was better.

The lesson that can be learned from this Everton team is that the simple way to goal is often the quickest and best. They had several good ball players in their side but never over indulged and concentrated instead on moving the ball forward with decisive and positive passes.

There used to be an old saying in football, 'Show me a good halfback line and I'll show you a good team.' In the modern language of today's game that would need to be altered to, 'Show me a good midfield trio and I'll show you a good team.' This was certainly true of Everton and when soon after my arrival as Derby County manager I teamed Don Masson and Bruce Rioch with Gerry Daly I was seeking the sort of midfield balance and bite that Kendall, Ball and Harvey used to provide at Goodison.

Arsenal 1970–71

Arsenal performed the FA Cup and League double exactly ten years after their neighbours and deadly rivals Tottenham but without ever winning the sort of praise that was lavished on that 'Super Spurs' side.

The Arsenal team, like the Leeds championship side of 1968–69, were superbly organized with a strong defensive foundation.

It was not until late in the season that they suddenly emerged as championship contenders, overhauling Leeds in the very last week after Don Revie's team had looked certain winners of the title. Five days after clinching the championship they showed their great character by going to Wembley and beating Liverpool in an FA Cup Final that went to extra-time.

Arsenal began to show champion style when Charlie George returned to the side after a long lay-off with a broken ankle. Playing just behind the front three

Arsenal's captain Frank McClintock is chaired by victorious team mates after the 1971 FA Cup Final.

116

strikers, he gave them the flair that had been missing from some of their performances. *I include them in this analysis of outstanding sides to show what can be achieved by giving a skilful individual player room for freedom of expression inside a tightly-organized team.*

There was a tendency for Arsenal to be almost mechanical and robot-like and they were involved in a lot of dour battles in which they wore the opposition down with a style that owed as much to sweat and stamina as skill.

But manager Bertie Mee and coach Don Howe wisely gave the creative George a fairly free rein and it was his gift for doing the unexpected that brought a new dimension to Arsenal's play.

The Arsenal line-up when they played Liverpool at Wembley, with Eddie Kelly coming on as substitute, was:

WILSON

RICE   McLINTOCK   SIMPSON   McNAB

STOREY   GRAHAM
GEORGE
ARMSTRONG   RADFORD   KENNEDY

Significantly it was George who struck a spectacular winning goal in extra-time.

The real strength of this Arsenal team was in defence, with goalkeeper Bob Wilson — whom I capped for Scotland — doing a magnificent job in covering for the weakness of both McLintock and Simpson in the air.

Frank McLintock marshalled the defence, his fine tactical awareness helping him make a successful switch from attacking wing-half to centre-half. He was helped by the expert covering of the composed Peter Simpson and the solid support of full-backs Pat Rice and Bob McNab.

Peter Storey played a Nobby Stiles type of game in front of the back line, winning the ball with fierce tackles and then getting rid of it quickly with simple but unimaginative passes.

Until the emergence of Charlie George, George Graham was the most creative of the Arsenal players. He had a deceptively casual looking style but had the football brain and passing ability to unlock the tightest of defences. His ability to climb for a ball made him a key man for Arsenal at set-piece situations both in attack and defence.

John Radford and Ray Kennedy were in harness together as twin strikers. Both were energetic, unselfish and powerful near goal. Radford preferred to shoot with his right foot, Kennedy with his left. They went together like bacon and eggs. They fed on the service of the remarkable George Armstrong who used to give Arsenal width and thrust by switching from one wing to another.

Armstrong was a master chipper of the ball and with a player of his enormous energy and stamina Arsenal were almost able to play a 4-3-4 formation!

There have been more attractive and entertaining Arsenal sides but I doubt if there has ever been one to match their efficiency and consistency.

Manchester United 1976–77

I suppose I could be accused of indulging myself for including the Manchester United team I guided to the FA Cup victory over Liverpool in this chapter on outstanding club sides.

What can be learnt from their achievement? In a word: CHARACTER.

The fact that they mastered the Liverpool team that won the League and later the European Cup is surely enough to rate them an outstanding side. That they did it at Wembley just 12 months after crashing to a demoralizing defeat in the FA Cup Final against Southampton speaks volumes for the team's determination and will power. And, yes, their great character.

After our defeat against Southampton – one of the biggest upsets in FA Cup Final history – I told my young side, 'We shall return.'

There was a touch of General MacArthur in my prophesy but I didn't have the American troops behind me! What I did have was a staff overflowing with talent and I was sure that the following season they would capture one of the major prizes.

I made only three changes in the team for our return visit to Wembley, and one of those – Arthur Albiston for Stewart Houston – was forced by injury. I brought Jimmy Nichol in to give us more artistry at right-back and bought Jimmy Greenhoff from Stoke in the certain knowledge that his creative touches and fine positional play would bring the best out of Stuart Pearson.

Our tactics for the Final against Liverpool were simple: be first to the ball . . . don't let them settle . . . attack their central defenders on their suspect left

The Cup goes to Tommy Docherty's head . . . Stuart Pearson and Lou Macari 'crown' manager Tommy Docherty after Manchester United's 1977 FA Cup Final victory over Liverpool. The United team had great character to go with their skill.

What it's all about ...The goal that won the FA Cup for Manchester United in 1977. Liverpool defender Phil Neal gives chase but too late to stop Lou Macari's shot going into the net off the shoulder of team-mate Jimmy Greenhoff. There was an element of luck about the goal but the foundation for it had been laid during training where United worked at opening up the heart of the Liverpool defence.

side . . . support each other and concentrate on playing football at all times.

We played a modified 4-2-4 formation, with wingers Steve Coppell and Gordon Hill just slightly withdrawn so that they could help pick up Liverpool dangermen Kevin Keegan and Steve Heighway:

STEPNEY

NICHOL   B. GREENHOFF   BUCHAN   ALBISTON

McILROY   MACARI

COPPELL   HILL

PEARSON   J. GREENHOFF

There were no cloggers in the team and I like to think that both United and Liverpool provided an advertisement for all that is best about British football.

What was particularly satisfying was that we got our two goals the way we had planned, by playing on the slight weakness we had observed in the centre of the Liverpool defence. As Emlyn Hughes hesitated, Stuart Pearson sprinted to fasten on to one of Jimmy Greenhoff's delicate flick passes and shot powerfully inside Ray Clemence's near post for the first goal.

Jimmy Case, Liverpool's man of the match by my reckoning, equalized within two minutes with a neat turn and a fierce rising shot. It would have crippled most teams but my boys had become men during the previous 12 months and it was their character that pulled them out of the crisis.

Just three minutes later Jimmy Nichol found Lou Macari with a neatly weighted pass. Macari skilfully headed the ball on down the middle of the Liverpool defence where we knew they were suspect. *Jimmy Greenhoff harrassed Tommy Smith as he attempted to clear the danger and the ball ran clear to Macari who had given everybody watching a lesson in the art of following up.*

He shot first time and the ball struck Greenhoff's shoulder and veered sharply past Clemence and into the net. There was an element of luck about the goal but the foundation of it had been laid on the training pitch where we worked at opening up the heart of that Liverpool defence.

Right through this book, you will find me making references to *character*. It is something of an indefinable factor. It is about a mixture of determination, endeavour, desire, and good moral fibre. You can only build it into your team by getting the players to adopt the right attitude of mind.

My Manchester United team had it in abundance. If I had had the chance to finish the job I started, I have no doubt that we could have gone on to even greater achievements.

Liverpool 1976–77

This was very nearly the *complete* team. With a dominating centre-half like Ron Yeats at the heart of the defence and a little more flair going forward they would have been the *perfect* team.

They had a finely judged balance of skill and strength, speed and stamina. And, of course, they had loads of character as they proved by winning the European Cup Final just four days after their defeat by Manchester United at Wembley.

Previous Liverpool teams – those managed by the irrepressible Bill Shankly – had more sparkle in attack but none matched the overall efficiency, organization and teamwork of this Bob Paisley combination.

In my opinion, Bob made just one mistake in what was an incredible season of success both for him and his team. He made Ian Callaghan substitute against United in the FA Cup Final.

I was convinced he would play Callaghan, with either David Fairclough or David Johnson wearing the No. 12 shirt. But Bob got it right for the European Cup Final, with Callaghan playing a key midfield role in the decisive victory over Borussia Moenchengladbach.

Liverpool were a more adventurous and imaginative team when tall John Toshack was fit to spearhead a 4-3-3 formation in which he and Kevin Keegan showed an almost telepathic understanding of each other's play. Toshack gave them goalmouth power in the air and was an easy target man to find. They were able to use more attacking variations when he was in the team.

With injury keeping Toshack on the sidelines, Bob Paisley decided to raid Europe with his team playing this 4-4-2 formation:

CLEMENCE

NEAL   SMITH   HUGHES   JONES

McDERMOTT   CASE   CALLAGHAN   KENNEDY

KEEGAN   HEIGHWAY

Keegan's deployment as a central striker proved a master tactical stroke by Paisley. He played what was probably the game of his life despite the close attention of West Germany's very capable defender Bertie Vogts.

With Keegan pulling defenders away from their central positions and Steve Heighway turning them inside out from the wings, the four midfield players were able to strike forward into the spaces created for them.

In European football the build-up tends to be slower and more deliberate than in English League games. This suited Liverpool ideally after the hectic pace of the FA Cup Final four days earlier. They played with great sophistication and style and fully deserved their 3-1 victory.

The lessons that can be learned from the performances of this Liverpool team are legion. They were well prepared for every match, organized but not to an extent where individuals were stifled and they got width in midfield by playing Ray Kennedy — brilliantly converted from striker — wide where his accurate left foot passes could disrupt unsuspecting defences.

They were composed under pressure, supported each other in all areas of the pitch and were masters of the quick break from defence. The 4-4-2 formation can be too defensive for my liking but played the Liverpool way with four attacking midfield players it can be devastatingly effective.

There is nothing too much wrong with British football while we can produce teams of this calibre. With just a little more spirit of adventure, they are the team that could help lead a great British revival.

7

Outstanding International Sides

Football has been my life for more than 30 years and in that time I have been fortunate enough to have played against and watched some of the greatest of all international teams. I have seen and studied the development of tactics that have gradually made teams more efficient but, generally speaking, less attractive to watch.

The danger of modern football, as I see it, is that sophisticated strategy could stifle the game. In my view the answers for the future lie somewhere between modern defensive tactics and the natural flair and artistry that used to shine through in the teams of the 'old school'.

Beckenbauer-inspired West Germany . . . Cruyff-driven Holland . . . Pele-propelled Brazil . . . these are the teams that have been closest to getting it right. But I go back more than 20 years for the international team that was possibly the greatest of them all . . .

Hungary 1953–56

I played for Scotland in the 1954 World Cup in Switzerland. The only major shock of the tournament was that Hungary failed to win it. They were far and away the best team among the 16 competing countries but, with key man Ferenc Puskas less than fully fit, they were beaten 3-2 by a competent but less adventurous West German team.

In the Final they were the victims of human failings, nerves and tension tripping them up in the match that really mattered after they had gone 33 games and four years without defeat.

The football world first started bubbling with news that this Hungary team was 'a bit special' after they had won the Olympic Games title in 1952. Amateurs in name only, they came to Wembley the following year and smashed England's undefeated home record with a stunning 6-3 victory. Six months later they provided even more damaging evidence of the demise of English football with a thumping 7-1 win in Budapest.

Imagine how I felt less than a year later when England handed out a 7-2 hiding to a Scottish team in which I was wearing the No. 4 shirt. Yes, that Hungary team really was 'a bit special'.

I got my first close-up view of them at Hampden Park in 1954 when they beat us 4-2. Five months later I was in the Scottish side startled to be leading

1-0 at half-time in the return match in Budapest. We hit the woodwork twice and Billy Liddell missed from the penalty spot and in the end the Hungarians won 3-1.

What struck me most about that Hungarian team was their ability to dictate the pace of a match. *They would deliberately slow it down in midfield to lure unsuspecting opponents into false positions and then whoosh! — they were away like the wild North wind.*

They played to a very flexible formation, with the players constantly changing positions. Nandor Hidegkuti wore a No. 9 shirt but played — quite baffling in those days — in a withdrawn position as the engineer rather than executioner of attacks. Hidegkuti developed as Hungary's schemer-in-chief after the richly talented Ladislav Kubala had defected to Spain. Even without Kubala the Hungarians were a mighty force, playing to a formation that could be loosely described as 2-3-1-4:

GROSICS

BUZANSKY   LANTOS

LORANT   ZAKARIAS

BOSZIK

HIDEGKUTI

BUDAI   CZIBOR

KOCSIS   PUSKAS

Hungary would switch from defence to offence with bewildering speed, the iniatiative being gained chiefly by the linking partnership of attacking right-half Boszik and Hidegkuti.

Wingers Budai and Czibor would drop back just a little deeper than inside-forwards Kocsis and Puskas, collect the ball and then dart down the touchlines like Olympic sprinters.

Hidegkuti was a really difficult man to mark. One moment he would be back on the edge of his own penalty area and the next racing upfront as the spearhead of the attack. Using these now-you-see-me-now-you-don't tactics, he helped himself to a hat-trick against England at Wembley.

Boszik, then a member of the Hungarian Parliament, was a dream of a right-half. His positional play was just perfect. He always seemed to be in the right place at the right time, whether it was to help out in defence or — more often — to take up space in the opposition penalty area as an extra forward.

Their passing movements made us British footballers feel as if they had come to our pitches from another planet. They would lull you into a false sense of security with a procession of quick, short passes that took them nowhere and then suddenly unleash a paralysing long pass that would arrive in space a split-second ahead of one of their 'tuned-in' team-mates.

They more than any team I have ever seen realized the importance of supporting runs. Every time a player was in possession he would have a minimum of two and sometimes as many as five team-mates getting into positions where they could receive the ball. It made it a nightmare for we defenders trying to work out who to pick up.

The two inside-forwards, Sandor Kocsis and Puskas, worked perfectly in harness. Puskas, with his heavier physique and his thundering left-foot shot, was the more effective of the two but Kocsis was more creative and artistic. He was also dangerous in the air and scored many spectacular headed goals, although in the main the team liked to play the ball quickly along the ground.

We in Britain had always sneered that the Continental footballers could not shoot for toffee. Well we all came unstuck against the Hungarians! Every one of the forwards was a crack marksman.

They had a better understanding than most international teams simply because they spent so much time playing together. Most of them were attached to the Honved (or Army) club of Budapest or to Red Banner.

The team broke up after the Hungarian uprising of 1956. I doubt if there have been more than three international teams to equal their brilliance since their reign as uncrowned champions of the world. It was a pleasure to play against them . . . even in defeat.

Brazil 1958

This Brazilian team that so spectacularly won the World Cup in 1958 revolutionized football by introducing the 4-2-4 formation. I briefly featured the team in the chapter on strategy but they are deserving of a much deeper analysis.

Their line-up for the 1958 World Cup Final in which they beat host country Sweden 5-2 was:

GYLMAR

D. SANTOS   BELLINI   ORLANDO   N. SANTOS

ZITO   DIDI

GARRINCHA   VAVA   PELE   ZAGALO

Brazil had failed in previous World Cup tournaments because nobody had been able to harness the skills of their stunningly talented individual players. In 4-2-4 they had come up with the perfect framework, keeping them organized but with sufficient freedom to do their own thing.

In a 4-2-4 system, the two linkmen are the vital cogs. They carry massive responsibility; if they are not functioning properly then the team can grind to a halt. Zito and Didi, the Brazilian midfield partners, were masters at their job.

Too many teams that copied the Brazil playing pattern flopped simply because their two men in the middle could not cope with the task of feeding the front four forwards and also covering in defence when needed. So gradually 4-3-3 evolved with three men sharing the work load in midfield and then came 4-4-2 as managers and coaches decided that too many out-and-out strikers was a luxury they could not afford.

Thinking back on that 1958 tournament, it is easy to see why 4-2-4 was doomed to a fairly short existence. It was Bill Nicholson, then England's coach and right hand man to Walter Winterbottom, who exposed the flaws in the system. He watched them annihilate Austria 3-0 in their first World Cup match and, with great tactical perception, worked out a way to stop them.

Right-back Don Howe patrolled in the middle of the defence, right-half Eddie Clamp played on the flank and left-half Bill Slater stifled Didi with disciplined man-to-man marking. *England cleverly cut off the Brazilian supply line and their negative but effective tactics earned a goalless draw against one of the greatest attacking teams of all time.*

It proved that 4-2-4 could be made a less than potent force by closing down on the two linkmen. Brazil quickly found a way round this in future matches by pulling Zagalo back into a withdrawn position, slightly ahead of the two link men but handily placed to help out in midfield if Zito and Didi were outnumbered. So almost as soon as the world were getting a first glimpse of the 4-2-4 system, Brazil were already gradually reshaping it to 4-3-3.

By the time of Brazil's successful defence of the World Cup in Chile in 1962, Zagalo's role was conspicuously that of a midfield player rather than a winger. He often dropped right back into a defensive position to cover for the veteran left-back Nilton Santos who had lost much of his pace and mobility, although still a master at positional play.

The line-up of the Brazilian team – minus the injured Pele – that beat Czechoslovakia 3-1 in the Final was:

GYLMAR

D. SANTOS   MAURO   ZOZIMO   N. SANTOS

ZITO   DIDI   ZAGALO

GARRINCHA   VAVA   AMARILDO

Possibly because of the absence of the injured Pele, Brazil were not as impressive in Chile as they had been in Sweden four years earlier.

But even with a more cautious approach, they were still the most powerful attacking force in the world and a lot of managers and coaches returned home from Chile with their thoughts tuned to the possibilities of football played the 4-3-3 way.

It is the Brazilian style of 1958 that I like to recall when thinking of football played at its most positive. Garrincha, Vava, Pele and Zagalo were all masters of ball control and I should not think there has been a more formidable forward line in the history of football, particularly when supported by linkmen Zito and Didi both of whom were geared totally to attack.

The 4-2-4 system can be operated properly only if you have players of the right quality. Brazil had the world-class footballers to make it work but even they had to concede that playing just two men in midfield left too many inviting gaps for the opposition. It is my favourite formation but whenever I send a team out to play 4-2-4 I instruct one or both of the wingers to drop back into deep positions whenever necessary.

Real Madrid 1956–60

I have included a club team in this international section because the marvellous Real Madrid side of the 1950s was virtually an international team. Among their stars were Argentinian Alfredo di Stefano, Hungarian Ferenc Puskas, Frenchman Rayond Kopa, Brazilian Didi (only for one season) and Uruguyan Jose Santamaria.

Real won the European Cup for the first five years of the tournament's existence, thanks largely to the consistently brilliant performances of di Stefano.

Like most people, I rated Pele the greatest of all forwards and for me Tom Finney was the outstanding British player of the last 30 years. But the player who gets my vote as the most *complete* footballer of them all is di Stefano.

He had a superb physique and was quick and well balanced. For a big man he was amazingly agile and could manoeuvre with the smoothness of a Nureyev even in confined space. He was the general of the Real team, basing himself just behind the front line from where he dictated play with a stream of intelligent passes.

There was not a weakness in his game. He was capable of having a shot at goal one minute, then emerging in his own penalty area the next minute to tackle for the ball. There is no such thing as a one-man team but Real came close to it with di Stefano, such was the dazzling dominance of the man.

He had a wonderful working relationship with Puskas, the two of them bringing the best out of each other with their positioning and tactical awareness. If di Stefano was the composer and arranger of the team, then Puskas was the lyricist. He was always on song when partnering di Stefano and scored a series of stunning goals by feeding off the artistic approach play of the Argentinian. Anybody lucky enough to have seen them share all seven goals in Real's dazzling 7-3 European Cup Final victory against Eintracht Frankfurt at Hampden Park in 1960 will surely share my view that there has rarely, if ever, been a two-man combination to match them.

Puskas scored four goals, slaughtering the Frankfurt defence with ferocious left foot shots. But it was di Stefano who was the superstar of the soccer stage, inventing magical movements with his midfield scheming and coming through to help himself to three goals.

The Real line-up for that memorable match was:

DOMINGUEZ

MARQUITOS   SANTAMARIA   PACHIN

VIDAL   ZARRAGA
di STEFANO
CANARIO   DEL SOL   PUSKAS   GENTO

The defence was organized round powerful centre-half Santamaria, with Argentinian international goalkeeper Dominguez as a formidable last line of defence.

But they were essentially an attacking side, with nearly everything revolving around di Stefano who almost arrogantly picked holes in a Frankfurt team that had destroyed Glasgow Rangers 12-4 on aggregate in the semi-final.

The graceful Del Sol formed a dangerous right wing partnership with Brazilian Canario but it was over on the left side that Real were at their most lethal. I have never seen a faster left winger than Gento who went past the Frankfurt defenders with such speed that they looked like statues. Puskas roamed on his inside like an assassin waiting to strike, while di Stefano strutted from one penalty area to the other demanding the ball and then using it with devastating effect.

The football they produced against Frankfurt was close to perfection and the roars of acclaim from the 127,000 Hampden Park crowd could not have been greater had Scotland been trouncing England!

England 1961

It is my personal view that the England team that won the World Cup in 1966 was not the best English international combination of the 1960s. The most efficient, yes, but not the best. At their peak, the Walter Winterbottom side captained by Johnny Haynes was the more skilful, adventurous and attractive.

Their most memorable performance — a nightmare memory for all Scots — came at Wembley in 1961 when they hammered Scotland 9-3. England were helped that day by a near-novice display from the Scottish defence.

Goalkeeper Frank Haffey was a bundle of nerves, the two full-backs Shearer and Caldow played both wide and square leaving centre-half Billy McNeill stranded in the middle without cover against the two-pronged attacks of Bobby Smith and Jimmy Greaves. Wing-halves Dave Mackay and McCann kept pushing recklessly forward with complete disregard for their defensive duties and left holes behind them that Johnny Haynes continually found with a procession of precise passes.

But Scotland's pathetic performance should not detract from the fact that this was an outstanding England team. They played to a fairly rigid 4-2-4 formation borrowed from the 1958 Brazilians:

SPRINGETT

ARMFIELD   SWAN   FLOWERS   McNEIL

ROBSON   HAYNES

DOUGLAS   GREAVES   SMITH   CHARLTON

The nine-goal savaging of Scotland was the fifth of eight mightily impressive displays in succession by that England team. They beat Northern Ireland 5-2, Luxembourg 9-0, Spain 4-2 and Wales 5-1. Then soon after the win against Scotland they massacred Mexico 8-0, drew 1-1 with Portugal in Lisbon and beat a very strong Italian side 3-2 in Rome.

England's success showed the value of keeping a settled side. Ten of the players were together in seven of the matches and this was reflected in their teamwork and in the results. In those eight games they scored 44 goals and conceded just 14.

I had some doubts about the stability of the defence under pressure but they had a fairly easy time during that 1960–61 season because the attack was continually dominating the matches. Bobby Robson and pass master Haynes worked smoothly and efficiently together in midfield, showing imagination with their positional play and their passing.

Tricky Bryan Douglas and the more direct and explosive Bobby Charlton were contrasting wingers who gave the England attack width, while in the middle Jimmy Greaves and Bobby Smith were putting the foundation to a partnership that was to flourish with Spurs the following season.

Greaves scored a hat-trick and Smith and Haynes each collected two goals in the rout of a Scottish side that was totally lacking in confidence and cohesion. In complete contrast to Walter Winterbottom's policy of keeping to the same nucleus of players, the Scottish selectors used 22 players in the three Home championship matches!

I fully expected England to make a convincing challenge for the 1962 World Cup in Chile but they were just a shadow of the side that had looked so impressive a little over 12 months earlier.

Bobby Moore, then a promising but raw 21-year-old, was drafted into the World Cup side in place of Bobby Robson. He played well but his style too closely resembled that of the other wing-half Ron Flowers. Neither of them were creative enough to give Johnny Haynes the support he needed in midfield and so England's 4-2-4 system failed to function properly.

I am sure Walter Winterbottom must often wonder what would have happened had the World Cup been staged a year earlier when England's players were at the peak of their form. At that time, they seemed good enough to win the World Cup.

England 1966

England won the World Cup without wingers and it started a trend that I feel did a lot of damage to British football. Too many clubs copied Ramsey's 4-3-3 system and suddenly wingers were a dying breed.

Without at least one winger in the attack, a team loses width and variety. It worked for England in the 1966 World Cup because they had players of the calibre of Alan Ball and Martin Peters who had the intelligence, speed and energy to use the wings, with fine overlapping support play from full backs George Cohen and Ray Wilson. But the clubs that blindly followed England's lead did not have players of this quality and many matches became bogged down in midfield, with nobody using the flanks to turn defences and get in around the back.

I'll ask a simple question to illustrate the point I am making. What would you normally do if you were locked out of your house and had lost the front door key? Answer: You would go down the side of the house and try to get in at the back.

Playing 4-3-3 without a winger meant that many teams were finding themselves locked out in the middle of the pitch but had nobody who could open the side gate and get in around the back way.

Whenever I send out a team to play the 4-3-3 way (which is often in League competition), I try to make sure that one of the front runners or one of the midfield players is a player with what I call 'wing sense'.

The days are of course long gone when a team could afford the luxury of having a winger standing out on the touchline uninvolved in the game until served with the ball to his feet. *Wingers must now be instructed to tackle back in midfield and deep in defence if necessary to help the team effort but when coming forward their main point of attack must be aimed down the flanks.*

Anyway, Sir Alf Ramsey's England team triumphed without a recognized winger in 1966. It was a marvellous performance that proved that Ramsey had few equals as a tactician.

A point that a lot of people tend to forget is that in the first three matches of that tournament, Ramsey selected teams that included a recognized winger. John Connelly played in the goalless draw against Uruguay, Terry Paine was on the right wing in the 2-0 victory over Mexico and Ian Callaghan took his place in the 2-0 win against France.

The 'wingless wonders' did not appear in the World Cup until the quarter-final match against Argentina. It was a system that had worked successfully in a one-off experiment against Spain in Madrid seven months earlier.

The England line-up for the final three matches on their way to the world championship was:

BANKS

COHEN   J. CHARLTON   MOORE   WILSON

STILES   R. CHARLTON   PETERS

BALL   HUNT   HURST

England laid the foundations for their victory over West Germany in the Final with their performance against Portugal in the semi-final.

The Germans were so impressed by the commanding midfield performance of Bobby Charlton that they over-reacted and sacrificed one of their most inventive players, Franz Beckenbauer, in an attempt to stifle Charlton's influence.

Beckenbauer was given the negative task of shadowing Charlton where ever he went. He was not decisive enough as a defender to shut Charlton out completely and West Germany lost his skilful support play when they were striking forward.

England were not the most creative and attractive team in the tournament. Hungary, Argentina and Portugal had more skilful and more imaginative players but collectively that was a superbly well organized England team with possibly a better defensive set-up than any other world championship-winning side.

Gordon Banks, Bobby Moore and Bobby Charlton were players of true world class. If you could have mixed the 1961 attack with the England defence of 1966 it would have produced a team to rival the best there has ever been.

Brazil 1970

From my frequent references to the attacking qualities of the Brazilian world champions of 1970 in previous chapters, you will have gathered that I was a great admirer of this team.

I based myself in Guadalajara during the group matches in Mexico and so was able to get a close up of the Brazilians in action. They were much more tactically aware than many people expected and played a flexible 4-3-3 formation, with Rivelino patrolling out on the left in midfield as a withdrawn winger:

FELIX

CARLOS-ALBERTO   BRITO   WILSON-PIAZZA   EVERALDO

CLODOALDO   GERSON

RIVELINO

JAIRZINHO   PELE   TOSTAO

The one thing we shall never ever know about this Brazilian team is the ability of their defence to stand up against sustained pressure. They often looked brittle at the back but were never really given a thorough testing. Perhaps it was because of the heat and the altitude but all the teams that faced them, with the exception of Peru, adopted a safety-first defensive attitude, dropping back into deep defence and conserving their energy for counter attacks.

Peru took them on in the quarter-finals and were rewarded with two goals but they had little defensive discipline themselves and conceded four goals against one of the greatest attacking teams that I have ever seen.

One of my favourite players in the attack was one of the least publicized – Gerson, who played just in front of the defence where he could always be found with a pass. Because he positioned himself so deep, opponents didn't mark him as tightly as he should have been and so he had the freedom to dictate the direction and pace of the play the moment he was in possession. He had great vision and the ability to hit a long ball to the exact right spot where the likes of Pele, Tostao and Jairzinho were waiting to pounce.

Gerson was the commander of the centre of the field, with Clodoaldo and Rivelino patrolling up and down either side of him. Rivelino was a sly fox out on the left, drawing a full-back out of position by taking him on a false trail in-field to leave room for left-back Everaldo to make an overlapping run. In the next attack he would come through on an orthodox left wing run, turning the full-back before firing over a precision left foot centre.

Jairzinho, Pele and Tostao were masters at creating space for each other by drawing defenders with decoy runs and often all three would set off on diagonal runs knowing full well that they would not be receiving the ball. As defenders chased to cover their movement, players would come through from behind to take advantage of the wide gaps that had been opened. One of the things that really struck me about Jairzinho, Pele and Tostao – all of them outstanding individualists – was their willingness to unselfishly 'sell themselves' to help the team effort.

I particularly remember the way Jairzinho took the experienced Italian defender Facchetti out of position with a dummy run in the 1970 World Cup Final. Brazil were cantering to victory with a 3-1 lead when the gifted Clodoaldo made a searching run from midfield, moving from right to left past three opponents with the ball at his feet.

Clodoaldo lured the right-back towards him and then released a pass into the path of Rivelino in space on the left. He quickly transferred the ball to Pele who made a pretence at racing towards goal. The Italian defenders, rapidly reorganizing themselves after Clodoaldo's run, braced themselves to try to block Pele's progress but were then further deceived and confused by the sight of Jairzinho moving at speed from the right wing to a central position as if in anticipation of a pass from Pele. Facchetti, one of the world's supreme left-backs, was completely taken in by this decoy movement and followed Jairzinho in a panic. Only then did he realize that right-back Carlos Alberto was up in support on the right wing. Pele calmly stroked the ball into unmarked Alberto's path and he struck a first-time shot just inside the far post.

It was the final goal of the 1970 tournament and fittingly captured the great attacking skill and the unselfish attitude of the Brazilian superstars.

They proved better than anybody that ball-playing individualists can still function without loss of impact or identity inside a well organized team structure. The likes of Pele, Jairzinho, Rivelino, Tostao and Gerson all did their own thing but never indulged themselves at the expense of the team.

Italy 1970

Italy were the most frustrating team of the 1970 World Cup. They reached the Final but without hardly ever touching their true potential as an attacking force. It would have been a defeat for football had they beaten Brazil with their negative defensive tactics.

The only time they showed just what they could achieve with a positive pattern of play was when they were forced to come out of their shell in the memorable semi-final against West Germany. They had just gone 2-1 down in extra-time and suddenly instead of playing eight men back they had to push players forward in a do-or-die attempt to stay in the match.

The Italians finally emerged winners by the astonishing score of 4-3 after 30 minutes of extra-time that left everybody breathless at the sheer pace and excitement of it all. Italy proved during those 30 minutes that they had an attack that could be paralysingly brilliant but they had the shackles of defence tightly back on for the Final against Brazil. This is how they lined up:

ALBERTOSI

CERA

BURGNICH   ROSATO   FACCHETTI
                    BERTINI
            MAZZOLA   DE SISTI
DOMENGHINI   **131**
         BONINSENGA   RIVA

Cera was the 'libero' or free-back, sweeping up at the back. Burgnich, Rosato and Facchetti lined up in front of him with Bertini patrolling the width of the pitch just ahead of them. De Sisti was also primarily a defensive player and Domenghini and Mazzola — both technically equipped for attacking play — were clearly under orders to give priority to defence if ever Brazil were in possession.

So in a World Cup Final, Italy played with just two strikers who ploughed a lonely path upfield. Both Boninsenga and the wonderfully talented Luigi Riva had the skill and speed to disrupt defences but time and again they were outnumbered because of Italy's reluctance to send players up in support.

It is significant that Italy reached the World Cup quarter-finals by scoring just one goal in three games. They had lost only one of 23 matches in their build-up to the tournament but any chances they had of winning the World Cup disappeared with their mania for defence.

Amazingly, they left one of their most gifted players — 'Golden Boy' Gianni Rivera — kicking his heels on the touchline for much of the tournament. He and team manager Feruccio Valcareggi were unable to communicate with each other and so Rivera was reduced to the role of a substitute, coming into matches too late to reveal the full range of his stunning ability as an attack-minded midfield schemer.

He was sent on for just the last six minutes of the Final against Brazil when all was lost. In my opinion he should have been in the team at the start of the match. Had he and Mazzola played side by side with orders to be progressive, the Brazilian defence might have been given a searching test.

I include the Italian team in this Chapter because I admired their technical skill. They were experts at passing, had excellent control of the ball even under the severest pressure and in Luigi Riva they had a truly outstanding striker. It's a great pity that they did not give him the support that he deserved.

What the Italians lacked most of all in Mexico was the right attitude. The squad that carried Italy's challenge to Argentina for the 1978 World Cup was at least as talented as their 1970 predecessors, yet they had still not completely rid themselves of the doctrine that football should be based on defence rather than attack.

Scotland 1974

I had a particular interest in the Scottish team that qualified for the 1974 World Cup Finals in West Germany. In my admittedly biased opinion, that was as well organized and efficient a Scottish side as there had been in recent years.

I laid the foundations for the team during my term as Scotland manager before moving on to Manchester United. *It was obvious that Scotland had the talent to reach the World Cup Finals. What I had to do was to instil the ambition.*

For too many years, the be-all-and-end-all for Scottish fans, administrators and even players had been to get the better of England in the Home Championship tournament. They were too parochial and blinkered in their outlook. I like to think I made them more internationally minded.

It took a lot of heart-searching before I handed over the reins of the Scottish team to Willie Ormond. I knew that he was inheriting a squad that included players who could propel Scotland into the World Cup Finals.

They were desperately unlucky to be eliminated without losing a match in their three qualifying group games. Yugoslavia and Brazil – both held to a draw by Scotland – qualified by virtue of having a better goal average than the Scots.

The game that cost Scotland a place in either of the two final groups was the one in which they beat Zaire 2-0. They needed at least another two goals against weak opposition but were below peak power in the penalty area where they lacked ideas and imagination.

When I was Scotland's manager, I based my tactics on a 4-2-4 formation in which the wingers accepted that they had a responsibility to drop back to assist in midfield or defence if we were under pressure.

The two key men around whom I had built the team were Martin Buchan in defence and Billy Bremner in midfield. Buchan's ability to read situations,

Martin Buchan...a composed and constructive central defender whose quickness of thought and action made him a key member of the Manchester United and Scotland defences.

his composure under pressure and his quickness of thought and action convinced me he was the man to hold the back line together. I appointed Bremner captain because I knew his driving leadership would inject confidence and enthusiasm into the players around him.

So it was particularly rewarding for me to see both Buchan and Bremner emerging as the mainstays of the Scotland team that performed with such credit but little luck in West Germany. Their line-up for the goalless draw with Brazil was:

HARVEY

JARDINE   HOLTON   BUCHAN   McGRAIN

BREMNER   HAY
DALGLISH
LORIMER   JORDAN   MORGAN

Kenny Dalglish cleverly operated between midfield and as a supporting striker to Joe Jordan, who proved his ability in the highest class with his determined running and his power in the air. Lorimer and Morgan both patrolled as withdrawn wingers, striking quickly from the touchlines when Scotland were in possession and tackling back to cover in midfield and defence when the ball was with the opposition.

David Harvey had a marvellous World Cup as a defiant last line of defence, working well with big Jim Holton. Full-backs Jardine and McGrain were both solid and reliable and quick to take the opportunity to make overlapping runs.

For me, that Scottish side incorporated all that is best about British football. They were positive, fearless, worked for each other and had strength in the air as well as on the ground. The manager who can marry the strengths of the British game with the superior individual technique of the Continentals will have a championship-winning team.

Holland 1974

The best team did not win the World Cup in 1974. In my view, runners-up Holland were the side that deserved to take the championship but they were mastered in the Final by a West German team that had better discipline and, it seemed, more *desire* to win.

Before the championship Finals started, Holland looked the best equipped side in the tournament. In such players as Neeskens, Krol, Van Hanegem and, of course, Johan Cruyff they had skilled individualists who could stand comparison even with the Brazilian superstars of previous World Cup tournaments.

But it was a star player who was *missing* from the Holland line-up in West Germany who possibly held the key to their failure to win the championship. Barrie Hulshoff, the powerful centre-half for Ajax, damaged a knee and to make up for his absence Dutch manager Rinus Michels pulled skilled midfield schemer Arie Haan back into the defence as an emergency sweeper. Hulshoff's

Johan Cruyff... always perfectly poised and aware of what is going on around him. It was his magical skills that steered Holland into the 1974 World Cup Final against West Germany.

injury robbed Holland of their usual soundness in defence and Haan's withdrawal into the back line meant they lacked full creative power in midfield.

Even so, I thought Holland overall were the best team in the tournament. Their line-up for the Final against West Germany was:

JONGBLOED

SUURBIER   HAAN   RIJSBERGEN   KROL

JANSEN   VAN HANEGEM   NEESKENS
CRUYFF
REP   RENSENBRINK

What was so refreshing about Holland – and West Germany, for that matter – was that they showed a positive attitude at the back of their defence. *Haan, Suurbier and Krol were always looking for the chance to advance as auxillary attackers so that when Holland were in possession they had as many as eight players coming forward. This support running is what 'total' football is all about.*

The thing that swung the balance of power West Germany's way was the outstanding performance of Bertie Vogts who gave a lesson in the art of man-to-man marking. He severely curtailed the threat of Dutch dangerman Cruyff who had done so much to steer Holland into the Final. Vogts was never far from Cruyff, cramping his style and his movement so that he was unable to give the Dutch attack their usual drive and direction.

Van Hanegem and Neeskens played superbly together in midfield but with Cruyff so closely marked they did not have the customary outlet for their passes. This resulted in many of Holland's passes being played square in the Final and this was no way to penetrate the West German defence.

Bertie Vogts tried the same man-to-man marking tactics against Kevin Keegan when playing for Borussia Moenchengladbach in the 1977 European Cup Final. Kevin got the better of him by taking him on and using his acceleration to get beyond him into the penalty area. Cruyff elected to try to outwit him by continual switching of positions but he rarely got away from Vogts for long enough periods to do any permanent damage.

West Germany 1974

The West German team that won the 1974 World Cup was just past its peak. I rated them at their most powerful and impressive two years earlier when capturing the European Nations championship, with Gunther Netzer in majestic form in midfield.

It was evident that they were functioning below their best when East Germany hurried and harried them to a 1-0 defeat in a qualifying group match, Jurgen Sparwasser going past Bertie Vogts Keegan-style to score the winning goal eight minutes from the end of a hectic game.

But they emerged as champions because they had enormous resolution and determination to go with their skills and, of course, the inspiring support of the home fans. They lacked the flair of the team that triumphed in Europe in 1972 but they had total commitment and their team organization and understanding was the best on display.

The team that beat Holland 2-1 in the Final was:

MAIER

VOGTS   SCHWARZENBECK   BECKENBAUER   BREITNER

HOENESS   OVERATH   BONHOF

GRABOWSKI   MULLER   HOLZENBEIN

Their style was the same as when conquering Europe in 1972 but Wolfgang Overath in midfield, although a skilful and polished player, did not have the inventive mind of Netzer whose almost arrogant scheming had given West Germany an exclusive touch of class.

Vogts, Schwarzenbeck, Breitner and Bonhof all had specific players to mark in

Kevin Keegan...using his great acceleration to get the better of his man-to-man marker Bertie Vogts during the 1977 European Cup Final between Liverpool and Borrusia Moenchengladbach. Vogts stifled Johan Cruyff in the 1974 World Cup Final but was given a chasing by Keegan.

the Final against Holland, with Beckenbauer operating as a sweeper-cum-schemer who was as usual constantly taking every opportunity to be progressive.

Uli Hoeness covered marathon distances as a midfield partner to Overath and a support striker to Muller. Grabowski and Holzenbein were clever and lively on the flanks, with the gifted Breitner often coming smoothly through as an extra man on the left.

Gerd Muller was not the frightening force he had been in the past but still retained his instinct for a half chance as he proved when skilfully swinging around in the penalty area to shoot the winning goal after collecting a marvellous pass out of defence from the enterprising Bonhof.

By reaching the Final with teams of all-purpose players, West Germany and Holland had pointed the way to the future.

They proved, as Brazil did in 1970, that outstanding individual players need not be stifled by organized teamwork.

In modern football, defenders must be distributors and attackers . . . attackers must be prepared to defend . . . and all players should be looking to support each other.

Yes, it's as simple as that.

8
World Cup '78

Whatever else the 1978 World Cup Finals may eventually prove they have shown that soccer, well organized and controlled, is probably the world's most attractive, and certainly the best loved team sport. What other game could have glued hundreds of millions of people throughout the world to their television sets night after night and, next morning, provided the basis for hundreds of thousands of conversations in which everyone and anyone can, and will, provide an 'expert analysis'? The whole of the South American continent was totally involved for weeks and the Argentine football authorities and general public deserve congratulations for their organization, control, and most of all for their infectious enthusiasm for the game.

Some cynics are suggesting that it was wonderfully convenient for the competition that Argentina reached the final, but where were they when the home side overwhelmed Peru to reach that position? They certainly could not have been watching the game, one in which strategy and tactics counted for little — all that was intended by the Argentinians was that they should score

Roberto and Gentile tangle for possession during the Italy/Brazil 3rd place playoff.

A jubilant Kempes celebrates his first goal in the final.

goals, and score they certainly did. Any team in the world would have been hard put to have resisted such pressure, both on and off the pitch, and the Peruvians, fellow South Americans, were perhaps the least well equipped of the teams left at that stage of the competition to handle such an onslaught. Tactically there were few lessons to be learned from the match, but it was certainly one of the most exciting I have ever watched and, in its simplicity of purpose, had much to recommend it to the student of soccer the world over.

Historically, too, Argentina's success is not without precedent. The host nation has a long tradition of performing well in the competition and it is not unheard of for them to win. West Germany, Brazil, even England will testify to that, and the Argentinians did at least change stadia during their run! Having said that, it was a pity that the home team, coming to the final with an almost unblemished record, should tarnish it somewhat in the last moments. One certainly keeps the challenger waiting in the boxing ring as a matter of course, but it is not really the done thing in the World Cup Final. Neither is it good manners to wait until the last moment to object to the weight of the gloves being worn! Holland's Rene Van de Kerkhoff had, after all, been wearing that protective plaster in the previous two games and there had been three clear days to lodge any protest. Both these actions smacked of managerial manoeuvrings on the part of the sad-faced Menotti and they certainly had an affect on the game when it eventually began. Faced by some eighty thousand vociferous fans, the odds are that any referee will shade his decisions in favour of the home side and, therefore, perhaps the tougher the game the better for that home side?

As for the game itself, it was certainly one of the most exciting and fiercest for many years. The Argentinians attacked as they had for almost all the competition, but the Dutch stood their ground and overall had much the greater share of the play — indeed in the second half they mounted long and sustained periods of pressure and must be considered unlucky losers. But, as in all sports, a little luck goes with the winning, and the Argentine team certainly had that — and, for my money, the most exciting player of the competition. Mario Kempes moving forward with speed, control and purpose is an exciting footballer, and his two goals underlined the difference between the two sides — Argentina had a star, Holland, alas, did not. What they did have was many fine players, a very high work rate, a total commitment to each other, and, probably the smoothest side in the competition — with Cruyff, they might have had the Jules Rimet Trophy as well.

Looking back on the competition as a whole, surprisingly little emerged as far as new strategy or tactics is concerned. There was certainly nothing as innovative as Brazil's startling 4—2—4 of 1958, or indeed as Ramsey's wingless wonders of 1966 — even Holland's total football of 1974 looked a little jaded four years later and somewhat strained when played on large pitches where the total involvement and support of all the players demand Herculean efforts of strength and stamina. Some general observations on a few of the games will perhaps give us food for thought.

Earlier in this book I spoke about playing to one's strength, and the Scotland/Peru match was, I thought, a case in point. Scotland began brightly, swinging the ball about, playing it wide, getting it into the middle in the air for a big centre forward, and driving through from the midfield. Great stuff, and rewarded by an early goal. Then suddenly it all began to go wrong. The drive from the midfield stopped, Rioch seemed to park himself in the Peruvian half and the passes became much more intricate, shorter and numerous. Perhaps they had watched too closely their opponent playing exactly this sort of game and been impressed. But what they had forgotten is that this is a South American strength: short, intricate passes in front of goal, the ball on the ground, and the final quick return ball for a fierce and

Joe Jordan makes a determined challenge and meets equally determined resilience from the Dutch captain Rudi Krol during Scotland's 3—2 victory.

A cool Willy Van der Kerkhoff plays the ball out of danger from the
pursuing Houseman.

usually swerving shot at the goal — effective and good to watch when played
properly, but hardly Scotland's strength.

At the other end of the park it seemed to me to be the same story in
reverse. Scotland's defence looked to be organized, strong and well-geared
to handling the typically British-type of aerial attack. But faced with a
complex, ground-mounted assault, bewilderment became the order of the
day, and those vital and constructive clearances from defence disappeared
from the Scots' repertoire. Scotland's next game is perhaps best forgotten —
confidence had gone, commitment and belief were missing and, against a
side which a few months earlier they would surely have hit for six, they
struggled to draw.

Then against Holland came a transformation. Faced with a European style
of play, Scotland reverted to type and played to their strength throughout
the match. In soundly beating the eventual runners-up came, for me, one
of the best goals of the competition. Archie Gemmill, with precious little room,
but with great skill and determination, coolly placed the ball in the back
of the net and did much to restore the team's spirit and pride in itself.

Another game which had much to commend it was that between France
and Argentina. I thought that the French were the unluckiest of the 'early
plane-catchers'. They played their football with a lot of skill and a surprising
amount of confidence for a side not usually reckoned to be in the top echelon
in recent years. However in the game against Argentina these skills looked to
be a little too fragile when faced by a team with great commitment and
enthusiasm and a referee not inclined to be over-protective!

The game for third place between Italy and Brazil had the dubious honour
of providing the most boring opening twenty minutes of the tournament.
But it did give us something to analyse and perhaps to put into practice. The
Italians were marking tightly — as they can do so well — not only the Brazilian
front men but the midfield creators as well. Not unnaturally this had the
effect of stifling the game. But it did show that when man for man marking

141

Luque, Kempes and Butoni celebrate Argentian success.

is taken this far, then space is not being marked. Once the players realize this it is up to them to play the ball into the spaces, either for a defender coming through the middle or a full back overlapping on the wings. When the Italians scored the game came to life and eventually gave us much good football, Brazil's two fine goals proving just too much for a weakened Italian side that had played some uncharacteristically attacking football for almost long enough in this competition.

What of the individual stars of Argentina '78? For me these include Rossi, Kempes, Ardiles, Brandts, Benetti, Neeskens, Dirceu, Amaral and Fillol. The brightest of these was surely Rossi, fast, graceful, skilful and brave and, despite being the recipient of many shuddering tackles, a sportsman. Kempes was the most exciting — one glimpse of a route to goal and he went for it with speed and considerable skill. Ardiles impressed with his controlled, well-groomed involvement, perhaps reflecting his physical appearance, and Benetti and Neeskens for their commitment and drive. In a tournament somewhat short of class defenders, Brandts and Amaral took the eye. Amongst an unimpressive crop of goalkeepers Fillol looked to be more competent than most, and Dirceu's vicious swerving goals, usually from very long range, were real show-stoppers.

One final accolade goes to the Argentine crowds. If they didn't know the words or tune for visiting sides' National Anthems, and most often they did not, then they stood, kept silent and applauded, and that is a lesson for all wherever the game is played.

Index

te: numbers set in bold type refer
illustrations

imovic, Jovan 15
: Milan FC 107
ax FC 12. 60, 134
berto, Carlos 130, 131
bertosi 13
biston, Arthur 118, 119
en, Les 104, 105, 107
en, Ronnie 93
naral, Luis 140
narildo 125
field (football ground) 72
diles, Osvaldo 140, 142
gentina 8, 15, 33, 72, 129, 132,
    140–1
mfield, Jimmy 127
mstrong, George 117
senal FC 7, 9, 10, 16, 54, 90,
    116–17
hurst, Len 76
tle, Jeff 88
ton, John 112
stria 55, 125
ay tactics 100–3

bington, Carlos 15
ck-heeling 33
ley 108
ker, Peter 104, 107
l, Alan 16, 59, 60, 69, 70, 115,
    116, 128, 129
nks, Gordon 8, 9, 51, 52, 54, 129
rlow, Ray 93
rnes, Peter, 22
seball Ground (Derby County FC)
    17
xter, Jim 108
yern Munich 60
ckenbauer, Franz 6, 14, 60, 63,
    99, 122, 136
l, Colin 99
l, Willie 114
llini 56, 124
nfica FC 112
rtini 131, 132
st, George 18, 22, 26, 112, 113
ngham, Billy 115
ackburn Rovers FC 115
anchflower, Danny 104, 105, 107
nd, John 109
nds, Billy 16
netti, Peter, 9, 60, 99
szik 56, 123
yce, Ronnie 104
yle, John 70

Brabrook, Peter 109
Brady, Liam 31
Brazil 10, 15, 43, 52, 56, 59, 60,
    122, 124–5, 130–1, 133, 134,
    137
Breitner, Paul 10, 136, 137
Bremner, Billy 7, 15, 70, 77, 96,
    114, 133
Brennan, Shay 112
Brito 130
Brooking, Trevor 31
Brown, Bill 104, 107, 109, 115
Buchan, Martin 12, 14, 72, 118,
    119, 133
Buckley, Steve 111
Budai 56, 123
Budapest 55, 123, 124
Bulgaria 58
Burgnich 131, 132
Burkett, Jack 109
Busby, Sir Matt 55
Buzanski 123

Caldow, Eric 127
Callaghan, Ian 15, 61, 120, 121, 129
Canario 126
Cantello, Len 88
captaincy 95–7
Carberry 108
Case, Jimmy 16, 39, 121
catenaccio 58, 60, 62, 63
Celtic, see Glasgow Celtic
central defenders 12–14
Chalmers, Seve 110
Channon, Mick 45
Chapman, Herbert 54
Charlton, Bobby 6, 8, 15, 26, 29,
    31, 34, 59, 60, 82, 99, 100, 102,
    112, 113, 127, 128, 129
Charlton, Jack 10, 59, 64, 80, 82,
    90, 97, 114, 129
Chelsea FC 24, 70, 76, 82, 90, 95
Cherry, Trevor 61
Chile 125, 128
chip passing 30–1
circuit training 24
Clamp, Eddie 125
Clark, John 110, 111
Clarke, Allan 77
Clemence, Ray 9, 14, 53, 61, 119,
    121
Clodoaldo 130, 131
Clough, Brian 8, 17
Cohen, George 11, 59, 128, 129
Collins, Bobby 31
Compton, Denis 108
Connolly, John 129
Cooke, Charlie 70
Cooper, Terry 10, 52, 60, 114
Coppell, Steve 11, 21, 22, 119

corner kicks 80, 81
Craig, Jim 110, 111
Crawford, Ray 59, 108
Crerand, Pat 88
Croy 88
Cruyff, Johan 18, 60, 122, 134, 135,
    176
Cruz 112
curled passes 33, 34
Currie, Tony 31
Czechoslovakia 84, 125
Czibor 56, 123

Dalglish, Kenny 72, 134
Dear, Brian 109
Del Sol 126, 127
Daly, Gerry 15, 16, 17, 116
defensive set-pieces 74–80
Derby County FC 8, 12, 16, 17, 19,
    22, 23, 24, 70, 100, 101, 107,
    116
Didi 56, 124, 125, 126
Docherty, Tommy 118
Domenghini 131, 132
Dominguez 126
Donachie, Willie 11
Douglas, Bryan 127, 128
Dunne, Tony 112
Dyson, Terry 104, 105, 107
East Germany 88
Eastham, George 31
Eintracht Frankfurt 126, 127
Elsworthy 108
England 29, 34, 43, 53, 55, 59, 64,
    66, 80, 99, 101, 108, 123, 127,
    128, 130
European Cup 11, 58, 60, 75, 82,
    110, 112, 118, 120
European Cup Winners' Cup 109
Eusebio 112
Everaldo 130
Everton FC 16, 17, 70, 115

FA Cup 7, 9, 12, 15, 16, 31, 70, 98,
    109, 116, 121
Facchetti, Giacinto 10, 63, 131, 132
Fairclough, David 98, 120
Fairs Cup 82
Felix 130
Feyenoord FC 58, 111
Finney, Tom 19, 20, 22, 34, 59
First Division (English) 8, 42
Flowers, Ron 127, 128
formations 54–62
Foulkes, Bill 112
France 129, 140, 141
France 129, 140
Francis, Trevor 61
free kicks 82, 84, 88, 89
full-backs 10–12

Gabriel, Jimmy 115
Garrincha 56, 88, 124, 125
Gemmell, Tommy 58, 110, 111
Gemmill, Archie 17, 141
Gento 126, 127
George, Charlie 18, 19, 116, 117
Gerson 15, 40, 130, 131
Giles, Johnny 15, 31, 77, 114
Glasgow Celtic 7, 11, 54, 58, 72,
    110–11
Glasgow Rangers 127
goalkeeping 9–10, 45–53, 76, 77,
    78, 93
Goodison Park (football ground) 16,
    116
Grabowski, Jurgen 99, 136, 137
Graham, George 90, 117
Gray, Eddie 114
Greaves, Jimmy 18, 34, 80, 106, 107,
    127, 128
Greenhoff, Brian 12, 19, 70, 119
Greenhoff, Jimmy 118, 119, 120
Greenwood, Ron 34, 60, 109
Grosics 123
Guadalajara 43
Gylmar 56, 124, 125

Haan, Arie 63, 134, 135
Hampden Park (football ground) 33,
    34, 55, 127
Hancock 59
Harmer, Tommy 76
Harris, Ron 95
Hartford, Asa 88
Hasil 58
Haynes, Johnny 31, 127, 128
heading 38–41
Hector, Kevin 51, 70, 99
Henry, Ron 104, 107
Herrera, Helenio 58, 110
Hidegkuti 56, 123
Highbury (football ground) 10, 104
Hill, Gordon 11, 21, 22, 61, 119
Hodgkinson, Alan 9
Hoeness 136
Hogan, Jimmy 55
Holland 12, 122, 134–6, 137, 139,
    140–1
Hollins, John 70, 82, 84, 90
Holton, Jim 134
home and away tactics 100–3
Honved FC 124
Hopkinson, Eddie 9
Houston, Stuart 118
Howe, Don 117, 125
Hudson, Alan 31
Hughes, Emlyn 14, 61, 120, 121
Hulshoff, Barrie 12, 134
Humberto 112
Hungary 8, 55, 122, 124, 129

Hunt, Roger 18, 45, 59, 129
Hunter, Norman 114
Hurley, Charlie 76
Hurst, John 115
Hurst, Geoff 14, 18, 19, 43, **53**, 59, 60, 101, 103, 109, 110, 129
Husband, Jimmy 115
Hutchinson, Ian 90

ideal players 7–22
Inter Milan 60, 63, 110, 111
interval training 24
Ipswich Town 59, 107, 108
Israel 58
Italy 40, 61, 131–2

Jairzinho 40, 41, 43, 52, 60, 85, 88, 130, 131
Jansen 135
Jardine, Sandy 11, 134
Jennings, Pat 9, 10, 33
Johnson, David 120
Johnstone, Jimmy 11, 110, 111
Jones, Cliff 104, 105, 107
Jones, Joey 121
Jones, Mick 114
Jongbloed, Jan 135
Jordan, Joe 134

Kay, Tony 115
Keegan, Kevin 19, 119, 120, 121, 136, **137**
Kelly, Eddie 117
Kempes, Mario 139, 140
Kendall, Howard 16, 70, 115, 116
Kennedy, Ray 16, 61, 117, 121
Kevan, Derek 76
Kidd, Brian 112
Kindvall 58
Kirkup, Joe 109
Kocsis 56, 123, 124
Kopa, Raymond 126
Kovacs, Stefan 60
Krol, Rudi 10, 134, 135

Labone, Brian 60, 115
Lantos 123
Law, Denis 18, 33, 80, **83**
Leadbetter, Jimmy 59, 108
League Championship, the 16, 59, 70, 114
Lee, Francis 29, 60
Leeds United FC 11, 70, 80, 90, 96, 114, 115, 116
Lennox, Bobby 110, 111
Leon 60
Liddell, Billy 123
Liverpool FC 9, 12, 14, 16, 23, 75, 82, 98, 107, 116, 117, 118, 119, 120–1
Lorant 123
Lorimer, Peter 33, 114, 134
Luton Town FC 11
Luxembourg 60, 127

Macari, Lou 15, 72, 119, 120
Mackay, Dave 104, 107, 127
Madeley, Paul 9
Maier, Sepp 9, **53**, 136
Maine Road (football ground) 9
Manchester City FC 9, 10, 56
Manchester United FC 7, 8, 9, 11, 12, 15, 16, 19, 22, 31, 70, 88, 98, 101, 112–13, 118–20, 132
Marciano, Rocky 23
Mariner, Paul 61
Marinho, Francisco 10

marking 64–7
Marsh, Rodney **57**
Masson, Don 17, 31, 100, 101, 116
Matthews, Sir Stanley **20**, 22, 59
Mauro 125
Mazzola 111, 131, 132
McCalliog, Jimmy 31
McCreadie, Eddie 82
McCreery, David 98
McDermott, Terry 61, 121
McFarland, Roy 12, **13**, 107
McGovern, John 17
McGrain, Danny 11, 134
McIlroy, Jimmy 31
McIlroy, Sammy 15, 119
McLintock, Frank **116**, 117
McNab, Bob 117
McNeill, Billy 110, 111, 127
Medwin, Terry 105
Mee, Bertie 117
Mexico 52, 60, 127, 129, 130, 132
midfield play 15–17, 67–70, 93
Moore, Bobby 8, 12, 14, 26, 43, 59, 60, 64, 101, **102**, 103, 109, 129
Moran 108
Morgan, Willie 134
Morrissey, Johnny 115
Mortimer, John 76
Mullen, Jimmy 59
Muller, Gerd 80, 136, 137
Mullery, Alan 60
Munich 109
Murdoch, Bobby 110, 111

Neal, Phil **119**, 121
Neeskens, Johann 134, 135, 136
Nelson, Sammie 108
Netzer, Gunther 136
Nichol, Jimmy 118, 119
Nicholson, Bill 104, 107, 125
Nicklaus, Jack 31, 40
Nish, David 11
Norman, Maurice 104, 107
Northern Ireland 33, 127
Nottingham Forest 8, 17
Nureyev, Rudolf 126

Octavio, Machado 15
off-side trap 92–3
O'Grady, Mike 114
O'Hare, John 70
O'Neill, Martin 17
Old Trafford 16, 88, 90
Orlando 56, 124
Ormond, Willie 133
Osgood, Peter 70, 90
Overath, Wolfgang 15, 103, 136, 137

Pachin 126
Paine, Terry 129
Paisley, Bob 120, 121
passing 28–34
Pearson, Stuart 9, 19, **39**, 70, **118**, 119, 120
Pele 6, 7, **8**, 18, 26, 27, 34, 40, 41, 52, 56, 80, 84, 88, 122, 124, 125, 130, 131
penalties 93–4
Peters, Martin 33, **52**, 59, 60, 99, 109, 128, 129
Phillips, Ted 59, 108
Peru 130
Poland 99
Portugal 8, 15, 127, 129
possession 41–3
Preston North End FC 7, 19, 34, 91, 93, 109

Puskas, Ferenc 56, 80, 122, 123, 124, 126, 127

Queens Park Rangers 17

Radford, John 117
Ramsey, Sir Alf 16, 22, 59, 99, 108, 128, 129
Rangers, see Glasgow Rangers
Rappan, Karl 58
Real Madrid
Rep, Johnny 135
Revie, Don 56, 114, 116
Rice, Pat 33, 117
Rijsbergen 135
Rioch, Bruce 17, 100, 101, 116
Riva, Luigi 131, 132
Rivelino 84, **86**, 88, 130, 131
Rivera, Gianni 15
Robson, Bobby 127, 128
Rocco, Nereo 58
Roker Park (football ground) 76
Rosato 131, 132
Rossi, Paulo 140, 142
Rowe, Arthur 115
Royle, Joe 115
Rumania 80

Sadler, David 112
Sandor 124
Santamaria 126
Santos, D. 56, 124, 125
Santos, N. 56, 124, 125
Schultz, Willi 62, 103
Schwarzenbeck 136
Scotland 33, 34, 55, 70, 72, 73, 122, 127, 132–4
Sealey, Alan 108
Sexton, Dave 24, 90
Shankley, Bill 120
Shearer 127
Shilton, Peter 9, **52**
shooting 34–7
shuttle running 24, 25
Simpson, Bill 110, 117
Sissons, John 109, 110
Slater, Bill 125
Smith, Bobby 18, 104, **105**, 107, 127, 128
Smith, Tommy 14, 75, 82, 120, 121
Southampton FC 7, 31, 118
Spain 123, 129
Sprake, Gary 114
Springett, Ron 127
Stamford Bridge (football ground) 82
stamina training 23–6
Standen, Jim 109
Stefano, Alfredo di 6, 18, 126, 127
Stein, Jock, 110, 111
Stephenson, Roy 59, 108
Stepney, Alex 9, 12, **52**, 112, 119
Stevens, Dennis 115
Stiles, Nobby 16, 59, 64, 66, 112, 129
Stoke City FC 19
Stokes, Bobby 31
Storey, Peter 16, 117
strategy 54–94
strikers 17–19
substitutes 98–100
Sunderland FC 76
Suubier, Wim 10, 135
Swan, Peter 127
Sweden 56, 59, 124, 125
sweepers 62–4
Swift, Frank 9
Switzerland 122

tackling 43–5
Tambling, Bobby 76, 82
target men 70–3
Thompson, Peter 60
Thomson, George 93
through passing 31, 32
throw-ins 89–92
Tilkowski, Hans 103
Todd, Colin 12, **13**
Toshack, John 19, 120, 121
Tostao 130, 131
total football 60, 63
Tottenham Hotspur FC 9, 104–7, 115, 116
training with the ball 26–53
Trautmann, Bert 9

Upton, Frank 76
Uruguay 128

Van de Kerkhoff, Rene 140
Van Hanegem 58, 134, 135, 136
Vava 56, 124, 125
Venables, Terry 82, 84, 95
Vernon, Roy 115
Vidal 126
Viktor 84, 85, 88

Wales 29, 72, 127
wall defence 77, 78, 79, 82, 84
wall passing 28, 29, 30
Wallace, Willie 110, 111
Webb, David 90
Wembley (football ground) 9, 15, 2?, 34, 55, 80, 93, 99, 101, 112, 1?, 117, 118, 120, 123, 127
West, Gordon 115
West Bromwich Albion FC 88, 93
West Germany 60, 61, 63, 99, 10?, 103, 121, 122, 129, 131, 132, 134, 136–7
West Ham United FC 16, 19, 34, 8?, 109
White, John 31, 104, 105, 107
White Hart Lane (football ground) 104
Whittle, Alan 115
Wilkins, Butch 61
Wilson, Bob 9, 117
Wilson, Ray 11, 59, 128, 129
Wilson-Piazza 130
wingers 19–22
Winterbottom, Walter 125, 127, 1?
World Cup 12, 15, 16, 22, 26, 33, 40, 43, 52, 56, 59, 60, 63, 64, 66, 84, 88, 99, 108, 122, 124, 125, 127, 128, 132, 138–142
Wright, Billy 7
Wright, Tommy 115

Yashin, Lev 9
Yeats, Ron 120
Yorath, Terry 77
Younger, Tommy 34
Yugoslavia 15, 133

Zagalo, Mario 56, 59, 124, 125
Zaire 133
Zakarias 123
Zarraga 126
Ze Maria, Jose 10
Zito 56, 124, 125
Zoff, Dino 9
Zozimo 125